SHERLOCK HOLMES's LONDON

SHERLOCK HOLMES's LONDON

EXPLORE THE CITY IN THE FOOTSTEPS OF THE GREAT DETECTIVE

ROSE SHEPHERD

To Bob, naturally.

Published in 2015 by CICO Books
An imprint of Ryland Peters & Small Ltd
20-21 Jockey's Fields
London WC1R 4BW
341 E 116th St
New York, NY 10029

www.rylandpeters.com

10 9 8 7 6 5 4 3 2 1

A CIP catalog record for this book is
available from the Library of Congress
and the British Library.

ISBN: 978 1 78249 257 3

Printed in China

Editor: Alison Wormleighton
Designer: Paul Tilby
Picture researcher: Claire Gouldstone
Map illustrator: Michael Hill

Art director: Sally Powell
Head of production: Patricia Harrington
Publishing manager and editor: Penny Craig
Publisher: Cindy Richards

PREVIOUS PAGES: page 1: A rainy day in
London, c.1903; page 2: The new Tower Bridge
from the south side of the Thames; page 3: Jeremy
Brett and David Burke as Holmes and Watson.

RIGHT: Fleet Street, once home of the British
national press.

OPPOSITE: New houses in London's crowded
East End.

CONTENTS

Introduction

"Under such circumstances I naturally gravitated to London, that great cesspool into which all the loungers and idlers of the Empire are irresistibly drained."

Dr Watson, *A Study in Scarlet*

OPPOSITE: Small ships and barges crowd Fresh Wharf in London's busy docklands.

The London of Sherlock Holmes is a city of the imagination. Arthur Conan Doyle did not extend himself in describing it. With a few deft pen strokes he gave us fog and gas lamps, hansom cabs, gentlemen's clubs and opera, pawnbrokers and gin palaces, wily street urchins and dull-witted "Scotland Yarders"—which, for us, the avid readers, is enough. We *know* that London of the 1890s, capital of Great Britain, of Empire and Commonwealth, in the last gasp of the Victorian era. We can see the teeming thoroughfares, the

horses drawing carts, landaus, broughams, the diffused glow from shop windows, the swirling "pea-soupers." We can hear the ring of iron horseshoes, the clatter of wheels on cobbles, the music of an organ-grinder, the cries of hawkers selling nostrums, matches, posies, whelks. It's a little bit edgy, dirty, smelly, but always exciting.

Nor has it all vanished. On the contrary, it is astonishing how much of today's London would be recognizable to Holmes and Watson. Here and there are survivors from the Middle Ages— remnants even of Roman times. Tudor black-and white abuts Jacobean grace and Georgian elegance, alongside 1960s Brutalism.

In the shadow of great towers of glass and steel are important public buildings of bygone ages,

ancient churches, impressive monuments, venerable hotels, restaurants, and stores. If we raise our eyes above plate glass and fluorescence, above nail bar and tanning salon, burger joint and mobile phone emporium, we see how handsomely historic London has accommodated the 21st century.

The very lack of unity makes for endless fascination. When the Great Fire of 1666 ripped the heart out of the medieval City, with the cinders still flying and the ground scorching underfoot, great men in powdered wigs began to draw up grand designs for rebuilding, with boulevards, avenues, and piazzas to rival the Baroque magnificence of Paris. Those plans never came to pass. Instead, today, we have a glorious gallimaufry, an architectural hodgepodge so full of surprises that the stranger can never quite guess what lies around the next corner.

We should remember also that, in Holmes's day, many of London's most iconic landmarks had appeared within living memory—indeed were in

OPPOSITE: Clogged artery. The traffic-choked Strand, where Watson stayed in a private hotel before his meeting with Holmes.

ABOVE: Crowd control. An upstanding London "bobby" wears the trademark London police helmet, introduced in the mid-1860s.

ABOVE: Work in progress. Begun in 1886, Tower Bridge was opened by the Prince of Wales in 1894. It was a marvel of its age, but not all commentators were impressed, damning it as "tawdry," "pretentious," and "absurd."

some instances garishly new and unassimilated. With the burgeoning population, wide roads, brash buildings, and urban sprawl, it must have seemed to Londoners that a whole new city had seeded itself and was springing up all around them, forcing itself upon the old.

In 1840 Trafalgar Square was laid out; Nelson's Column went up three years later ("a great national eyesore," complained *The Times* of London.) The Palace of Westminster, three decades in the building, was not completed until 1860. Tower Bridge opened in 1894 to mixed reviews. It had, opined the *Pall Mall Gazette*, "a subtle quality of ungainliness, a certain variegated ugliness"—it was "our ugliest public work." Who would have guessed back then how many tourists would flock to see it and take selfies on it?

In this book we set out upon a tour of the London of the world's first consulting detective. We visit his haunts and walk the streets in his footsteps, admire stupendous edifices, poke into nooks and corners and back alleys. We can shop, as he would have done, for snuff, shooting sticks, game birds for the table, fine wine, top hats, swords, and country tweeds. We can venture into his favorite restaurant and onto his crime scenes, and find out where justice was dispensed and where the villains whom Holmes brought to book would have languished.

The sharp-eyed will spot 19th-century street furniture—the 1,500 or so gas lamps maintained by five lamplighters that still illuminate benighted byways and Royal Parks; ornamental railings; pillar boxes, including the hexagonal "Penfold," bearing Queen Victoria's "VR" cipher; stone troughs where London's hardworking horses could take a drink; the public lavatories (mostly closed or converted) where grateful Victorians could "spend a penny."

But a city is more than just a built environment, it is a milieu, it is its people—or, rather, its people are its lifeblood. London in the late 1800s was home to four and a quarter million souls. It was a city of extremes of rich and poor: carriage folk in their Regency mansions, the poor in workhouses and slums, the destitute in rags, under arches, and an emerging middle class colonizing the Victorian pattern-book redbrick terrace homes (row houses) that are such a large part of current housing stock.

Masters, servants, wharfingers and wherrymen, shopkeepers, laundresses, flower girls, pen-pushers,

ABOVE: Life was no bed of roses for the Victorian flower girls. Most were Irish, many mere children. They eked out a living selling buttonholes and posies, dossing in slum quarters around Covent Garden, moved along by the police.

LEFT: JW Penfold's hexagonal pillar box, with decorations of acanthus leaves and balls, was introduced in 1866. This one is a replica installed in 1990 on Shad Thames at the foot of the stairs at the south end of Tower Bridge.

publicans, costermongers, cabbies, stable boys, actors, loafers, beggars, harlots, hucksters… All human life was here, giving voice to what Tennyson called "the central roar," and Robert Louis Stevenson "the low growl" of London.

Here too, of course, were the criminals whose vile pursuits furnished Doyle with such rich material. Most infamous of all was "Jack the Ripper," the fiend who stalked the squalid streets of Whitechapel. While he still exercises the minds of investigators who speculate as to his true identity, he remains a faceless figure, almost a figment.

By contrast, Sherlock Holmes, a character of fiction, is entirely real and present. Let us now get on his case.

HOW TO USE THIS GUIDE:
ELEMENTARY HINTS AND TIPS

"It is a hobby of mine," said Holmes, "to have an exact knowledge of London." Even in dense drizzle and fog, when Watson had lost his bearings, "Sherlock Holmes was never at fault… he muttered the names as the cab rattled through squares and in and out by tortuous by-streets."

The Edinburgh-born Arthur Conan Doyle, however, was less familiar with the great metropolis. He visited London relatives as a schoolboy—and retained a schoolboy's memories, patchy and imprecise. (Years later he would say that he had never visited Baker Street; he had simply forgotten.)

After studying medicine in Edinburgh, then working as a ship's surgeon, running a medical practice in Hampshire, and studying ophthalmology for two months in Vienna, in 1891 Doyle took lodgings in London at 2 Montague Place, behind the British Museum. He leased a consulting room at 2 Upper Wimpole Street with a share of a waiting room, and set up in practice as an eye doctor. He could go on foot from home to work, and "with never a ring [of the doorbell] to disturb my serenity," dashed off the early Sherlock stories at a prodigious speed. Later that same year he gave up both his practice and his lodgings to concentrate on writing, and moved with his wife, Louisa (Touie), and their infant daughter, Mary Louise, to suburban South Norwood. A son, Arthur Alleyne Kingsley, was born in 1892, but a marriage blessed with two children was blighted by Touie's ill health—in 1893 she was diagnosed with the tuberculosis that would kill her in July 1906.

It is no secret that Doyle used the London Post Office Directory and street atlases to plot Holmes's movements about town, whether dashing across a bridge to the badlands on the south side of the Thames or boarding a train for some outlying destination in search of the home of the dastardly Baron Gruner, and Appledore Towers, where Charles Milverton, "king of blackmailers," was shot dead—and serves him right!

In this book we concentrate on the London that Doyle *did* know, the Sherlock Holmes home turf, within a narrow compass of the West End, before venturing west and east and making sorties to the pleasanter destinations surrounding London.

Chapters 3, 4, and 5 are laid out as a series of walks, in distances that are indeed walkable, but we do not suggest pounding the pavements all day.

OPPOSITE: Sir Arthur Conan Doyle in 1909, the year his second wife, Jean, gave birth to a son, Denis. "He is a splendid chap!" wrote Doyle, who was then nearly 50, to his mother. "Such dignity! And such a head!"

RIGHT: The BBC's Sherlock (Benedict Cumberbatch) emerges from the café next door to "221B Baker Street" in the episode "The Sign of Three." Fans come from all over the world come here to take photographs, eat breakfast, and buy Speedy's memorabilia.

Apart from a manageable amble from Charing Cross to St Paul's, we propose being selective.

In Chapter 3, From Bloomsbury to Barts, for example, you might enter the nation's foremost museum, to emerge hours later, head spinning, and seek refreshment in a significant pub or sandwich bar, or soak up the sunshine in a pleasant green space. Devotees of the BBC's *Sherlock* would do well to start with breakfast at his favorite café, then stroll down to Russell Square, before taking the Underground for a visit to St Bartholomew's Hospital. For anyone with Holmes's scientific curiosity and sangfroid, the Hunterian Museum and Barts Pathology Museum would be complementary.

A quick scan of the maps will show that routes run within a short hop of each other, enabling you very readily to plan your own itinerary (setting off from St Paul's, say, to the Old Bailey, to Barts—or just taking the Tube from Baker Street to Barts). For exact locations and distances, use the postcodes and websites given in the List of Places (page 155). London is there for you. Only have fun.

A WORD OF CAUTION FROM THE EDITOR

Every effort was made to ensure the accuracy of what follows, but it seems some printer's devil has been up to mischief with this text. Strewn through it are 36 references to the Sherlock Holmes stories, some in plain sight and blameless, some cunningly concealed and deliberately misleading. No prize is offered to the sharp-eyed reader who spots them all; you must be content, as Holmes himself would have been, with a quiet glow of satisfaction (but answers are given on page 154). So come, come, the game's afoot!

CHAPTER 1

The Tale of the Mysterious Cloak

FOG, HANSOM CABS, AND FOUR-LEGGED FRIENDS

"It was a foggy, cloudy morning, and a dun-colored veil hung over the house-tops, looking like the reflection of the mud-colored streets beneath."

Dr Watson, *A Study in Scarlet*

OPPOSITE: Hansom cabs being driven through overcast London streets in around 1903. Cab drivers—and their horses—had to work in all weathers.

It is a gloomy, chilly dawn, and Londoners are waking to find the streets, for the fourth day, swathed in fog. From the Gothic Revival clock tower at the Palace of Westminster, Big Ben, the sonorous voice of London since 1861, sends shudders through the ether as it bongs out six. Magisterial, incontrovertible, the great bell, cast at London's Whitechapel Bell Foundry and weighing nearly 14 tons, is the city's principal timekeeper. The mechanism that drives the tower's four precisely synchronized clock faces is a triumph of the horologist's art, accurate to within a second.

The night cabs are just turning in, the weary horses grateful to be fed and bedded down on peat. In a couple of hours, if they're "working double-tide," the vehicles will have been cleaned and will be out on the road again, hired to day drivers, with fresh horses—weather permitting. In affluent homes across the city, maids are firing up the stoves. In the cozy sitting room at 221B Baker Street, the scuttle has been filled, the grate cleaned, coals laid—because Mrs Hudson's gentlemen lodgers like to draw up their fireside chairs as they chat over the *Daily Telegraph*. Wisps of smoke drift from domestic chimneys. Once the wheels of industry start turning, with factories' giant brick stacks belching filth, and steam trains and boats set in motion, conditions will be perfect for a "pea-souper."

A really bad 19th-century fog, wrote the meteorologist LCW Bonacina, "appeared early in the morning as a thick white mist, like the country fog, only dirtier. With the lighting of the fires it would soon become yellow and pungent, irritating the throat and eyes, till [by] midday the continued outpouring of chimney products would have turned the fog a sooty brownish black causing the darkness of night."

In his Sherlock Holmes short stories, Sir Arthur Conan Doyle made surprisingly few references to that peculiarly noxious phenomenon, the "London particular." However, he laid the fog on so thickly in *A Study in Scarlet*, and even more in *The Sign of Four* (when, what with the poor visibility and the

pace of travel, Watson quite lost his bearings), that we have forever in our minds an impression of an all-pervasive pall obscuring the dreary houses of London stock brick. And it was real enough, a toxic smog that blanketed the world's largest and most powerful metropolis, very different from the "white wool" fog that Holmes and Watson encountered on Dartmoor in *The Hound of the Baskervilles*.

In *The Adventure of the Bruce-Partington Plans*, the fog, so monotonous and oppressive, was almost a protagonist, playing on the nerves of the restless Holmes and swallowing up Arthur Cadogan West on the way to the theater with his fiancée, Miss Violet Westbury, when visibility was so bad that a cab was useless.

How lowering it must have been to awake morning after morning to an outlook so murky that often it was necessary for men to walk with flares in front of the omnibuses. Choking, stinking fog insinuated its way under doors and through cracks. It begrimed the buildings and blackened the leaves, obscured the view, obliterated the sky, extinguished the stars. It was a killer, too, in more ways than one, coating the lungs and claiming the lives of the frail and susceptible and of the hapless who blundered into canals and under vehicle wheels, or whose cab or omnibus careered off the road.

It was a gift to the opportunist thief, the "blagger," the "flimp" or snatcher, the "bludger," the "mug-hunter," and the violent and murderous criminal who could do a swift "Cadogan West" and melt away into the vile haze. Just as much, it was a gift to the Victorian writers of mysteries, ghost stories, and thrillers, evoking an atmosphere of menace, portraying London, "the Smoke," as at best sinister and at worst the Seventh Circle of Hell.

The causes and very nature of London smog were incompletely understood. "It looks partly as if it were made of poisonous smoke," related the art critic John Ruskin in 1884. "Very possibly it may be: there are at least two hundred furnace chimneys in a square of two miles on every side of me. But mere smoke would not blow to and fro in

ABOVE: From an upper-floor room at the Savoy Hotel, Claude Monet painted a series of views of Charing Cross Bridge in the fog, with trains streaming over the rigid metal structure, and with the Houses of Parliament seeming to evaporate in the background.

that wild way. It looks more to me as if it were made of dead men's souls—such of them as are not gone yet where they have to go."

For the American writer Nathaniel Hawthorne, London fog was "more like a distillation of mud than anything else; the ghost of mud, the spiritualized medium of departed mud."

Lost souls? The ghost of mud? Not to the eye of the artists who found that the fog softened and etherealized the harsh cityscape. For the American

James McNeill Whistler, it clothed everything "with poetry, as with a veil, and the poor buildings lose themselves in the dim sky, and the tall chimneys become *campanile*, and the warehouses are palaces in the night."

When the Impressionist painter Claude Monet arrived in 1899 to stay at the Savoy, where he captured the river view from his upper-floor window, it was with the express desire to paint the industrialized, polluted city. "In London, what I

love above all is the fog," he said. "It is the fog that gives it its magnificent breadth. Those massive, regular blocks become grandiose within that mysterious cloak."

Where prosaic souls such as Watson saw "yellow," these artists perceived more subtle chromatic shifts. When the color "London Smoke" was added to the *Artists' Encyclopaedia,* the advice was to mix two parts burnt umber with one part yellow and one part red.

For certain of the natives there was an element of the comic. If the official motto of the City of London is *Domine dirige nos* ("Lord, guide us"), the unofficial motto of the East Ender is "You've gotta laugh." In 1880, in *London Fogs,* while bemoaning the threat that it posed to health and morale, the Hon. R Russell acknowledged that smog "may be upheld as a nebulous and mysterious witticism, a gigantic piece of national humor, an enormous practical joke, and we cannot dispute the plea that it may be a source of amusement to the passing acquaintance."

There were those who even took perverse pride in this singularly British blight—"London's ivy," Charles Dickens called its fogs. The writer Blanchard Jerrold, on a London pilgrimage with the artist Gustave Doré, reported, "I could tell my fellow traveler that he had at last seen one of these famous darknesses which in every stranger's mind are the almost daily mantle of the wonderful and wonder-working Babylon."

The wonderful and wonder-working Babylon. The London of Sherlock Holmes.

CALL ME A HANSOM!

If the fog in the tales of Sherlock Holmes seems pervasive, the hansom cab is positively ubiquitous. Two types of cab, in a variety of styles, plied the streets of the capital: the two-wheeled hansoms and the four-wheelers such as the Clarence, nicknamed the "growler" for the noise it made over the cobbles. According to figures in the Metropolitan Police Commissioner's reports, 3,500 cab-masters held an annual license for somewhat fewer than 12,000 cabs, of which only

a small proportion would be on the road on any given day.

At the same time, we learn from *The Horse-World of London* by WJ Gordon (published in 1893—you can read it online, but it may break your heart) that there were 15,336 licensed cab-drivers, of whom "about 14 percent were convicted during the year for offences ranging from cruelty to drunkenness, in addition to those convicted of the minor offences of loitering and obstruction and including most of these there was a large percentage appearing on the masters' books as having proved themselves untrustworthy."

While the cabs were subject to yearly inspection, the cabbies faced only an initial examination, to

OPPOSITE: Designed by Joseph Hansom, a Yorkshire architect, the hansom cab had a sprung seat at the back for the driver, while two passengers, perhaps three, would sit inside. The cabs were light enough to be drawn by a single horse.

ABOVE: The hansom cab's maneuverability was a great advantage in London traffic jams, but passengers were discouraged from using them by uncertainty over the fare. Here a horse-drawn bus carries an advertisement for a penny rail fare.

demonstrate their knowledge of the city's topography. Their appearance, integrity, and character were their own affair.

We understand from this that Holmes and Watson chanced their luck in entrusting their safety to cabbies. In addition, the reason for the defensive attitude of John Clayton of 3 Turpey Street, the Borough, whose cab was out of

Shipley's Yard near Waterloo, in *The Hound of the Baskervilles*, becomes apparent. A "rough-looking" fellow, he nonetheless valued his livelihood and reputation. "I've driven my cab this seven years and never a word of complaint. I came here straight from the yard to ask you to your face what you had against me."

The London cab trade, WJ Gordon tells us, was in decline, while passenger rail, tram, and omnibus use was increasing. In 1888 there were 7,396 hansoms and 4,013 four-wheelers; four years on, though they remained a significant presence, there were 20 fewer hansoms and 92 fewer four-wheelers—not a dramatic fall, but the shape of things to come. One problem for the traveling public was uncertainty over cab fares; with train, tram, and omnibus you knew what you were in for, with no awkwardness over a tip.

The half-sovereign—ten shillings, half of one pound sterling—that Holmes promised Clayton in return for information must have been welcome indeed, with the hire of both horse and cab to be paid for (say, 18 shillings a week at the height of the season, and no less than nine shillings in the off-season).

There were 600 cab stands in London, with space for around 11 cabs at each. Four-wheelers served the train stations. When not on the stands, cabs went around, laden or empty, clogging up the highways and byways. The empty cabs—the "crawlers"—were a nuisance to everyone except those, such as Sherlock Holmes, who might at any moment wish to hail a passing hansom.

ALL THE PRETTY HORSES

The preferred color for cab horses was brown (bay or chestnut), and most were mares. They cost about 30 shillings when in the peak of condition, at about four years of age, and were shipped in mostly from Ireland, from the green turf of Waterford to the tarmacadam, the hated asphalt, the granite slabs and cobbles, and the timbers of London roads. After the trauma of the sea crossing they spent a couple of months recovering

and being trained for their employment, after which they were good for maybe three years before being sold on to haul tradesmen's carts.

Cab horses were well fed and watered, and they had to be. On a busy day they might cover 40 miles (64km), hauling half a ton of cab and driver, not to mention the portly Victorian gentlemen who might pile into the conveyance.

It was no use being sentimental and forming attachments. Some cab-masters merely assigned their horses numbers, though usually they were perfunctorily named. WJ Gordon cites, by way of example, three horses bought on a dirty morning and named Mud, Slush, and Puddle; four bought on a rainy day and called Oilskin, Sou'wester, Gaiters, and Umbrella; and three bought in hot summer and dubbed Scorch, Blister, and Silver Blaze. According to Gordon, "Some masters drive their own cabs, and naturally take good care of their own property; but with the bulk of the cabmen the horse is a machine, hired out as one might hire out a tricycle, and returned in a sufficiently sound state to avoid comment."

The 15,000-odd cab horses in service, of course, were only a small part of the four-legged army that kept the wheels of London turning. In 1891, Gordon tells us, an average of 92,372 vehicles entered the square mile of the City of London in any 24 hours, and though some of these, being cabs and omnibuses, might have been counted more than once, this is a fair indication of the scale of the comings and goings.

As Gordon so vividly expresses it, "It takes over 300,000 living horse-power to move the wheels along the roads of London, and if we were to stand the horses in single file they would reach along the bridle-ways from St Paul's to John o' Groats [in the Scottish Highlands, a distance of 690 miles (1,110km)].

There were tram horses, omnibus horses, dray horses, carriage horses, mail horses, hauliers' horses, rag-and-bone men's nags, undertakers' horses, barge horses, military steeds… Public

ABOVE: You can lead a horse to water… The Metropolitan Drinking Fountain and Cattle Trough Association was set up by philanthropists Samuel Gurney, MP, and barrister Edward Thomas Wakefield in 1859 to ensure that Londoners, man and beast, could slake their thirst.

transport alone required 50,000 horses to move the populace around every day.

Apart from the potential for jams, there were the hazards of reckless or drunken drivers, bolting or fallen horses, and issues of right of way, which inevitably led to accidents, injuries, and road deaths—there were 200 fatalities a year on average, with ten times as many maimed or injured. Remember how, in *The Hound of the Baskervilles*, Stapleton's cab, driven by John Clayton, "flew madly off down Regent Street," with Holmes, on foot, dashing off in wild pursuit amid the stream of traffic, too late to get the cab number? That Clayton should have been arrested! Then, as now, there was never a policeman around when you wanted one…

In addition, what of the risk to public health from the tons of horse manure deposited on the highways, turning to sludge in wet weather, blown around as dust in parching-hot summer, or attracting swarms of flies? Disintegrating hardwood roads, though preferred by the horses, were particularly problematic and noisome when spattered with dung.

The air of London was sweeter for the presence of Sherlock Holmes, but when it came to horse droppings, it was the crossing-sweepers and the boys with shovels who cleared paths for pedestrians. The Augean stables were nothing compared with London in the late Victorian period. As fast as the dung was transported by train and barge or horse-drawn wagon to outlying farms, it would be replenished. Farmers and market gardeners who would once have paid for manure at a rate of threepence a horse were reluctant to part with so much as a farthing, a quarter of one penny, for a commodity in such copious supply, and many stables were obliged to pay for its removal.

LEFT: Vehicle for advertising. The omnibus companies could make a shilling a day for product promotion. An average 14 passengers would be aboard at any time, but although, as we see, the buses served Baker Street, Holmes and Watson were never among them.

The year 1894 was known as that of the "Great Manure Crisis." Cities around the world had the same concerns. In 1898 the challenge was discussed at an international urban planning conference in New York City; no one had an answer.

Yet a solution was just around the corner. O bliss! O poop-poop! Oh my, oh my! The motorcar was coming, along with electric trams and motor buses.

In 1903, Sir Arthur Conan Doyle, by this date immensely rich, with Holmes brought back from the dead, bought himself a brand-new Wolseley with dark blue livery and shiny red wheels. He had a near brush with death when he managed to turn it over on top of himself and his brother Innes, turning into his driveway at his Surrey home. Undaunted, in April 1905 he won a time trial at the wheel, covering a distance of two miles and 1,500 yards (4.6km) in just under ten minutes.

Clearly Doyle had caught the bug. That September, at Folkestone Magistrates' court in Kent, he became one of the first motorists to pick up a speeding fine (£10), for whizzing along Cheriton Road at 26 miles per hour (42kph)—and owned up to a previous offence in Guildford, Surrey. There is always a policeman around when you don't want one.

AND TODAY...

The visitor to modern London is extremely unlikely to encounter a London particular—just London particulates. Various schemes are in force at the time of writing to reduce harmful vehicle emissions in the capital. Bicycles can be hired from and returned to docking stations around the capital, for those confident or intrepid enough to mingle with the traffic.

The horse world of London is a kindly and civilized one. Mounted police, the Household Cavalry, and recreational riders on Hyde Park's Rotten Row present a pleasing spectacle.

London cabbies with their black cabs, heirs to the hansom drivers, regulated by the Public Carriage Office, are these days for the most part civil and efficient, their brains bulging with "The

ABOVE: Sweeping up at Covent Garden market. Rotting cabbage leaves were as nothing compared with the droppings produced by a city so dependent on its horses, culminating in the "Great Manure Crisis" of 1894—but change was in the air.

OPPOSITE: The internal combustion engine revolutionized transport and transformed the city. The wealthy Sir Arthur Conan Doyle was one of the first to become the proud owner of a motorcar—and also one of the first to be fined for speeding.

Knowledge," a detailed familiarity with street routes and visitor destinations that earns them their license. There is no more demanding training course for taxi drivers in the world, taking an average 12 attempts and 34 months to pass. Gone are the old curmudgeons who would sometimes, against the rules, respond with a curt "I don't go south" when requested to cross the river. In Holmes's day a trip south invariably meant trouble; now, south London is increasingly gentrified and trendy.

If you plan to use public transport, an Oyster Card, a plastic smartcard, can be loaded to give pay-as-you-go credit on bus, Tube, tram, DLR, and London Overground rail. The world, as they say, is your oyster.

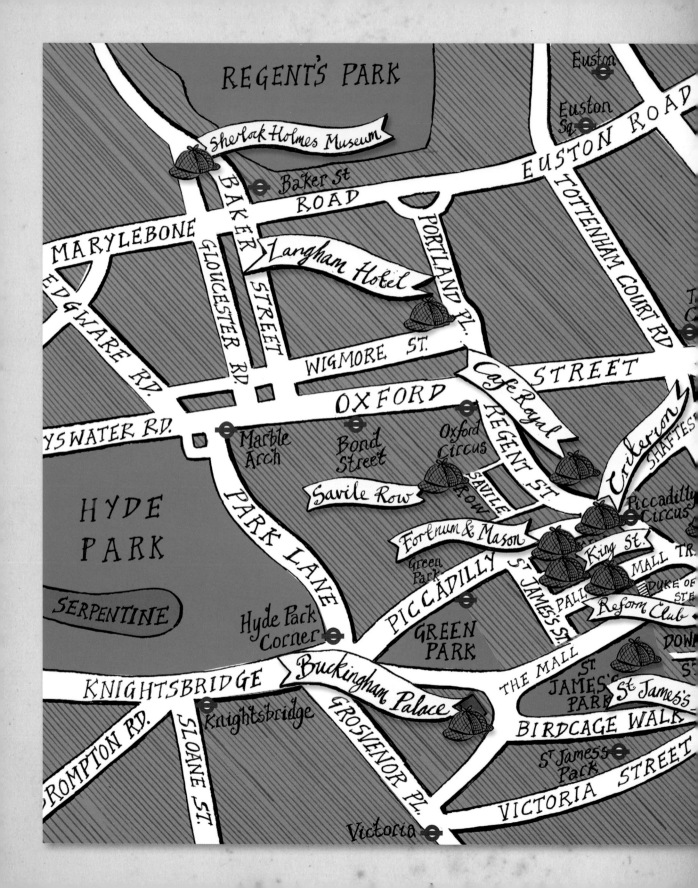

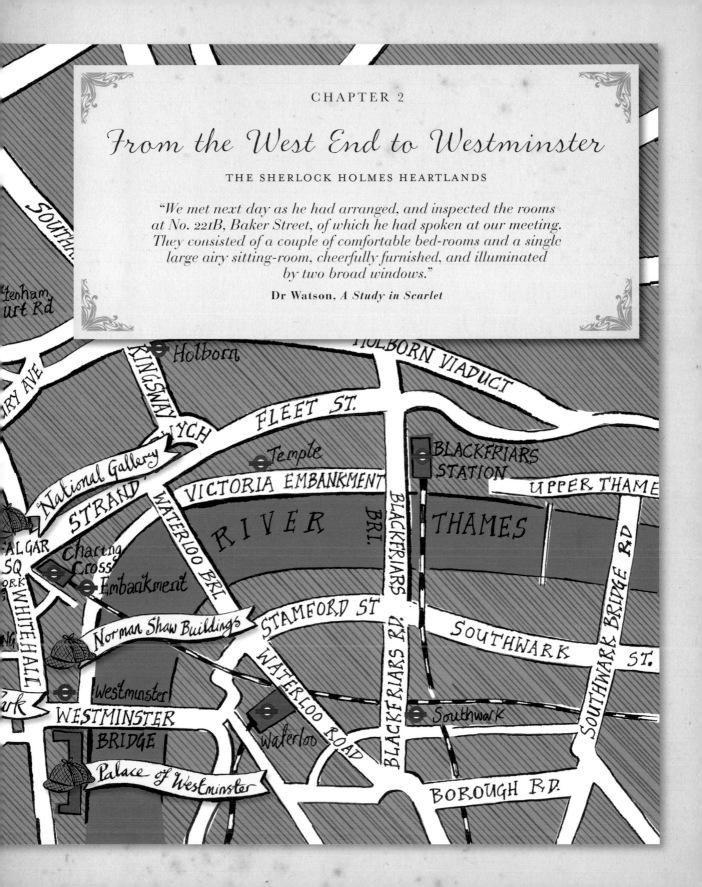

CHAPTER 2

From the West End to Westminster

THE SHERLOCK HOLMES HEARTLANDS

"We met next day as he had arranged, and inspected the rooms at No. 221B, Baker Street, of which he had spoken at our meeting. They consisted of a couple of comfortable bed-rooms and a single large airy sitting-room, cheerfully furnished, and illuminated by two broad windows."

Dr Watson, *A Study in Scarlet*

LEFT: Unveiled in March 1990, a blue plaque at the Sherlock Holmes Museum commemorates the great detective's years at one of the world's most famous addresses. The Georgian townhouse was indeed a boarding house in the late 19th century.

OPPOSITE: With the creation of Sherlock Holmes, Arthur Conan Doyle put Baker Street on the map. As a boy he had visited the waxworks of Madame Tussaud, then on Baker Street, as well as the London Zoo, at the northern end of Regent's Park.

At Christmas 1874, a 14-year-old schoolboy visited London for the first time, staying by turns with relatives at Earl's Court and Maida Vale. In a whirlwind three weeks, Arthur Ignatius Conan Doyle was taken to London Zoo in Regent's Park, to the Crystal Palace, the Tower of London, St Paul's Cathedral, and Westminster Abbey. He saw the Shakespearean actor Henry Irving in *Hamlet* at the Lyceum Theatre—but what must have made the most lasting impression were waxwork effigies at the museum of Madame Tussaud, and especially the Chamber of Horrors. "I was delighted with the room of Horrors and the images of the murderers," Arthur wrote to his mother, Mary. Today the waxworks gallery is around the corner on Marylebone Road, but in the 1870s it was on a road that Doyle would go on to immortalize—Baker Street.

Any tour of Sherlock Holmes's London must begin at the legendary **221B Baker Street**, where Holmes lived from 1881 to 1904. At that time there was no such address—nor, of course, would a street door be marked "B" (a discreet brass plate by the bell-pull might have read

"Sherlock Holmes, consulting detective; John Watson, FRCS") but we won't obsess on trifles as Holmes did.

Five lines serve Baker Street Station, among them the Metropolitan, the world's oldest underground train line, opened in 1863. A Sherlock Holmes silhouette suggests a shadow thrown up on the station's tiled walls. Emerging onto Baker Street you are met by a statue of the caped detective, courtesy of the Abbey National Building Society. Following the reassignment of street numbers in the 1930s, the Abbey occupied a building on what had been 215–229 Upper Baker Street, and employed a full-time secretary to deal with the correspondence that poured in from around the world, addressed to Sherlock Holmes.

Turn right and cross the road to reach the **Sherlock Holmes Museum**, marked 221B, which, sitting between 237 and 241, should properly be numbered 239. The upstairs rooms are presented as a Victorian bachelor pad cluttered with Holmes's possessions—his pipes, his magnifying glass and violin, his books and scientific instruments—while jolly costumed characters are on hand to make you welcome and

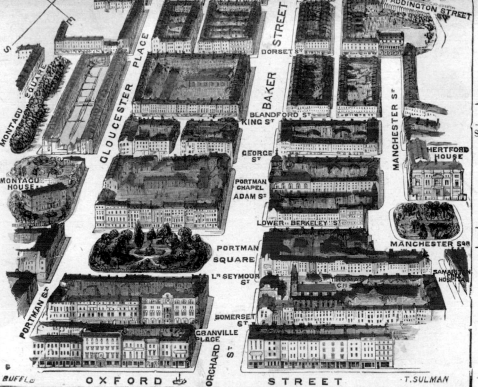

St. John's Wood.
LORD'S.

LORDS C.C.
CLERGY ORPHAN ASYLUM
ST. JOHNS CH.
BAPTIST COLLEGE
ZOOLOGICAL GARDENS
Regent's Park.

ST. JOHN'S WOOD RD.
MET. STA.
ST DUNSTANS VILLA
REGENT'S PARK

NORTH BANK
REGENTS CANAL
SOUTH BANK
ALPHA ROAD
CANAL
OUTER CIRCLE
PARK ROAD

ROYAL BOTANIC GARDENS
INNER CIRCLE
SOUTH VILLA

GREAT CENTRAL HOTEL & RAILWAY TERMINUS.

Marylebone Road.

Baker Street.

BLANDFORD SQR
HAREWOOD SQR
DORSET SQ
MILTON STREET
UPPER GLOUCESTER PLACE
UPPER BAKER ST.
YORK TERRACE
MET. STA.
BAKER ST. STA.
STA.
TUSSAUDS EXHIBITION

York Gate.

MADAME TUSSAUDS

Marylebone Road.

Baker Street.

GT. QUEBEC ST.
MARYLEBONE ROAD
DAVID ST.
YORK ST.
CRAWFORD ST.
BAKER STREET
DORSET ST.
MARYLEBONE WORKHOUSE
ST MARYLEBONE BURYING GROUND
PADDINGTON STREET

MONTAGU SQUARE
GLOUCESTER PLACE
BLANDFORD ST.
KING ST.
MANCHESTER ST.

George Street.

Charles Street.

ST. JAMES' CATHOLIC CH.

MONTAGU HOUSE
GEORGE ST.
PORTMAN CHAPEL ADAM ST.
HERTFORD HOUSE

Seymour Street.

LOWER BERKELEY ST.
MANCHESTER SQR

Lower Seymour St.

PORTMAN SQUARE
LR. SEYMOUR ST.
CH.
SAMARITAN HOSPITAL

PORTMAN ST.
SOMERSET ST.
GRANVILLE PLACE
ORCHARD ST.

Oxford Street.

OXFORD STREET

Oxford Street.

RUFFLE
T. SULMAN

BAKER STREET

FROM OXFORD STREET TO REGENT'S PARK AND ST. JOHN'S WOOD

to answer questions. There is a wealth of period detail—a bathroom with decorative ceramic basin and lavatory, Dr Watson's room with thumbed and dog-eared textbooks, and, amid the fireside chairs and trappings of a bachelor life, Mrs Hudson's more feminine room with a pretty fireplace.

North of Baker Street is Regent's Park, and the London Zoo, where the schoolboy Arthur Doyle "saw the animals being fed and the seals kissing their keeper"—but we are going the other way.

Baker Street itself is choked with traffic, being on 13 different daytime bus routes—but this is London. Heading south, take a left onto Wigmore Street, as Holmes and Watson did on their way to the Alpha Tavern in *The Adventure of the Blue Carbuncle*. You cross Welbeck Street, where, in *The Final Problem*, Holmes had to jump for his life to avoid being mown down by a two-horse van. (South of this is Vere Street, where a brick lobbed

from a rooftop shattered at his feet.) You are passing through the "doctor's quarters" of Wimpole Street, Harley Street, and Cavendish Square, where, as Dr Percy Trevelyan complained in *The Adventure of the Resident Patient*, a specialist would need substantial capital to pay enormous rents and furnishing expenses, besides hiring a presentable horse and carriage. It is the same today—but for the horse and carriage.

A left at Langham Place, leading to Portland Place, brings us to the **Langham Hotel** (No. 1C). Built in 1863–5 and opened by the Prince of Wales, the Langham was the largest and most up-to-date hotel in London, with 600 rooms, 300 lavatories, 36 bathrooms, and the first hydraulic lift in Britain. It was, then, the natural choice for the King of Bohemia, who stayed there under the alias Count Von Kramm in *A Scandal in Bohemia*. A strapping 6 feet 6 inches (2m) tall, with "the chest and limbs of Hercules," wearing a cloak of deep blue lined with flame-colored silk, fur-topped boots, and an eye mask, the king, visiting incognito, naturally did not want to draw attention to himself.

LANGHAM HOTEL
PORTLAND PLACE
LONDON W.

RIGHT: Fit for a king. The Langham was London's most modern hotel when it opened in 1865. This was where a tall man in cloak and mask checked in under the alias Count Von Kramm when seeking Holmes's help—anxious to avoid a scandal in his native Bohemia.

In 1889 Doyle was entertained at the hotel, along with Oscar Wilde, by Joseph Marshall Stoddart, managing editor of the Philadelphia-based *Lippincott's Monthly Magazine*. The two writers, much encouraged, went their separate ways, Doyle to write *The Sign of Four* (in which Captain Morstan checked in at the Langham Hotel, only to go missing, leaving behind some clothes and books, and curiosities from the Andaman Islands), Wilde to write *The Picture of Dorian Gray*. (The claim that the tradition of afternoon tea was born at the Langham's Palm Court would perhaps have surprised Anna Russell, Duchess of Bedford, usually credited as the "inventor" in the 1840s of that civilized English repast.)

South now down Regent Street, where Holmes and Watson shadowed the disguised Stapleton in *The Hound of the Baskervilles* before he gave them the slip in a hansom cab. A right turn onto Conduit Street brings us to the top of Savile Row, synonymous with the finest in men's tailoring.

CLOTHES MAKE THE MAN

Doyle gives us few insights into Holmes's sartorial style beyond Watson's comment that "he affected a certain quiet primness" of dress. What we *think* we know—and it is a tenacious conviction—is that he wore a deerstalker hat. Nowhere in the text does it say he did. On the other hand, nowhere does it say that he *didn't*. Sidney Paget, illustrator for *The Strand Magazine* (who modeled Holmes on his brother Walter), portrayed him in one. The actor William Gillette played him in one, onstage and in a silent movie (pages 91 and 149), and it is almost impossible to picture that thin, hawk-like Holmes profile without it. (Holmes's calabash pipe, it is said, was another Gillette innovation; thanks to its curly shape he was able to speak while holding it between his teeth—a straight pipe would have wagged about.) We *do* know that both Holmes and Watson sported those caped daytime coats known as "ulsters" with cravats. And in *The*

Red-Headed League we find Holmes in a pea jacket, a boxy, eight-button seaman's coat with slash pockets to warm the hands and large lapels to protect the ears from chill blasts. In the Royal Navy, where it is standard issue, it is called a "reefer." Entirely practical, then, but not the coat of a dandy.

Around the Baker Street apartment we hear of Holmes often in a dressing gown—blue, purple, or "mouse"—and in Persian carpet slippers. His wardrobe extended, for the purposes of disguise anyway, to the broad black hat, baggy trousers, and white tie of a nonconformist clergyman.

Where Sherlock shopped for his clothes, we can only hazard, but for the dedicated follower of male fashion, **Savile Row** is a great place to start. If Holmes or Watson could pass by here with us, they would recognize **Henry Poole & Co.,** "the founders of Savile Row," at No. 15. A family business begun in 1806 as a specialist in military tailoring, Henry Poole can claim to have created the original tuxedo. It received royal warrants from Napoleon II in 1858 and Queen Elizabeth II in 1976. Its list of past customers includes the Victorian novelists Charles Dickens, Wilkie Collins, Sir Edward Bulwer Lytton, and Bram Stoker; the former Prime Minister (and novelist) Benjamin Disraeli; the actor Sir Henry Irving; King Ferdinand I of Romania; Emperor Haile Selassie of Ethiopia; King Alfonso XIII of Spain; and Wilhelm Gottsreich Sigismond Von Ormstein, Grand Duke of Cassel-Felstein, King of Bohemia.

If Sherlock was not the Savile Row type, brother Mycroft, with his role in government, indeed was. At our first sight of him in the episode "A Study in Pink" from the BBC's *Sherlock*, he was wearing a three-piece tailored suit from **Gieves & Hawkes** at No. 1. In the Crimean War the enterprising James Gieve sailed to Sebastopol aboard a floating tailor's shop to offer his services as a military tailor, and in the 1880s he became sole owner of Gieves & Co. Thomas Hawkes, a military hatter, set up shop at No. 1 in the early years of the 20th century. The companies merged in 1974. Among their military lines are some splendid swords and scabbards.

At Vigo Street we swing back onto Regent Street, following its graceful curve to the **Café Royal**, across the road at No. 68. It was outside here that—who could forget?—Holmes was set upon by two men with sticks in *The Adventure of the Illustrious Client* before the assailants escaped by racing through the building into Glasshouse Street. What a shame he had not armed himself at Gieves & Hawkes, for wasn't he "an expert singlestick player, boxer, and swordsman"?

Opened in 1865 by a French wine merchant, the Café Royal was, by the 1890s, the haunt of a modish set who quaffed Veuve Clicquot while gilded mirrors reflected their beauty back and forth to infinity. What they would have made of hoodlums

BELOW: Pin sharp. Creator of the BBC's hit series *Sherlock*, Mark Gatiss, as brother Mycroft, sports a succession of smart tailored suits. Here he seems dressed for his day job of being in government—if not, indeed, *being* the government

: The glamorous Long Bar of the Criterion seems an unlikely place for a chance meeting between a down-on-his-luck Watson and Stamford, which was to lead to an introduction to Sherlock Holmes, new lodgings, and a new life.

tearing through, brandishing cudgels, is anybody's guess. The legendary Grill Room with its fabulous Louis XVI detail, gold-leaf ceiling and moldings, has been renamed the Oscar Wilde Bar, for it was here, in 1891, that Wilde fell for Lord Alfred Douglas, his "Bosie." Douglas was the author of the lines "the love that dare not speak its name." It is a far cry from "High Society afternoon tea" at the Café Royal to hard labor in Reading Gaol, which was to be the fate of Wilde just four years later.

The **Criterion** on Piccadilly Circus has happier associations, for it was here, while standing at the bar, that Watson felt a tap on his shoulder and, turning, saw young Stamford, in *A Study in Scarlet*. Opened in 1874, the Criterion is a study in opulence, a neo-Byzantine extravaganza. Purchase a glass of champagne in the Long Bar and you will be buying more than just a drink. For one thing, this was where, with a chance meeting, *it all began*.

SHOPPING WITH SHERLOCK

In *The Adventure of the Noble Bachelor* Holmes ordered the delivery of a lavish spread: "…a quite epicurean little cold supper," related Watson, "began to be laid out upon our humble lodging-house mahogany. There were a couple of brace of cold woodcock, a pheasant, a *pâté de foie gras* pie with a group of ancient and cobwebby bottles."

Despite quite frequently suggesting lunch or dinner at a restaurant, Holmes was no great eater. "His diet was usually of the sparest… to the verge of austerity," as we learn in *The Adventure of the Yellow Face*. Anorexia has even been suggested. But he pushed the boat out in anticipation of a visit from Lord St Simon, so wounded by Hatty Doran, his absconding bride, in *The Adventure of the Noble Bachelor*.

And from where had Holmes ordered such a feast? **Fortnum & Mason** suggests itself; we find it by turning right onto Piccadilly and proceeding west. Fortnum's is famous the world over for its hampers, and was in Holmes's day trading from a shop on the same site as the present neo-Georgian store, built in 1926–8. It was begun in 1707 by William Fortnum, a royal footman in the court of Queen Anne, and in the mid-19th century was in the forefront of a trend for picnic foods. "Look where I will," wrote Charles Dickens of Derby Day, "I see Fortnum & Mason hampers fly wide open and the green downs burst into a blossom of lobster salad!" Inventor of the "Scottish egg" (or scotch egg—a hard-boiled egg wrapped in sausage meat, then crumbed and deep-fried), Fortnum's was the first British grocer to stock Heinz Baked Beans, in 1886. They may even have stocked honey from Holmes's hives when he retired.

Farther west on Piccadilly we turn left onto **St James's Street** for some more discreetly smart shops that would have been known to Holmes—and, indubitably, to brother Mycroft.

As Holmes confessed in *The Sign of Four*, he had been "guilty of several monographs," one of them, "Upon the Distinction between the Ashes of the Various Tobaccos," in which he enumerated 140 forms of cigar, cigarette, and pipe tobacco, with colored plates illustrating the difference in the ash. Although a recreational smoker of pipe and cigars, puffing away at the strongest black tobacco, Holmes must have found his researches into tobacco ash demanding, as he dragged upon those 140 brands of cigar, cigarette, and loose tobacco—flake cut, ribbon cut, navy cut, shag. And where did he go for his smoking needs? Probably, as Oscar Wilde did, to **James J Fox** at No. 19. Holmes and Watson passed right by here on their way to visit Mycroft in *The Adventure of the Greek Interpreter*, entering Pall Mall at "the St James's End."

There has been a purveyor of tobacco, cigars, and smokers' paraphernalia here since Robert Lewis set up shop in 1787, and James J Fox has been in the business since 1881. In the Freddie Fox Museum (entry free) there is "possibly the last remaining box" of Luis Marx cigars, dating from 1898, along with the oldest box of Havana cigars in the world, and a High Court letter to Oscar Wilde showing a balance outstanding of seven shillings and three pence.

On dangerous missions, Watson might, at Holmes's behest, carry his service revolver, but the detective himself owned at least one pistol, with which to pock the walls at Baker Street in the interests of forensics research. Had he need of a firearm or more ammunition, he would have hastened to **William Evans**, then on Pall Mall, now on St James's Street at No. 67A, specialists in rifles, guns, and shooting clothes.

When it came to Chinese porcelain, Holmes knew his Hung-we from his Yung-lo. He had no difficulty in recognizing, in *The Adventure of the Illustrious Client*, eggshell pottery of the Ming dynasty. "It needs careful handling, Watson… No finer piece ever passed through **Christie's.**" We turn left onto King Street to find that esteemed auction house—founded by James Christie in 1766 on Pall Mall, and occupying a Renaissance-style Portland stone building at No. 8 since 1823.

In *The Adventure of the Three Garridebs* the eccentric collector Nathan Garrideb confided that he occasionally drove by Christie's and Sotheby's—but otherwise didn't get out much. All lots can be seen online at christies.com and once the sale is on view you can visit the salesrooms to take a look at that eggshell Ming vase that so interests you—then experience the nerve-racking drama of a live auction (ID required). Go in, go in—go on!

"This hat is three years old," says Holmes in *The Adventure of the Blue Carbuncle*. "These flat brims curled at the edge came in then. It is a hat of the very best quality. Look at the band of ribbed silk and the excellent lining. If this man could afford to buy so expensive a hat three years ago, and has had no hat since, then he has assuredly gone down in the world."

With the aid of a magnifying glass, the detective was able to deduce much from a stranger's battered black hat—his large brain (cubic capacity), grizzled hair, brand of hair cream—but what surprises is his acquaintanceship with fashion, not, surely, for fashion's own sake, but for what it could reveal. With no men's style journals to consult, he must have browsed the shops, and would have found what he needed at **James Lock**, at No. 6, St James's Street. The oldest hat shop in the world, it was established in 1676. The premises were originally an alehouse known as The Feathers, then a watchmaker's, then home to a maker of plaster figures, before James Lock took on the lease, moving across the street from west to east in 1765. If you want a really well-made tweed deerstalker, a top hat, or a bowler, they are here—at a price. For a hard hat, your head will be measured with a "conformateur" device; no assumptions will be made regarding brain size.

Then, if Holmes would study shoes for his monograph on the tracing of footsteps, **John Lobb** ("The most beautiful shop in the world," in the view of *Esquire* magazine) is at No. 9, the shop having opened in 1866.

When Holmes drank wine it had to be a good one: a bottle of Montrachet with cold partridge in

ABOVE: If you want to get ahead… James Lock, the world's oldest hat shop, could have furnished Holmes with a deerstalker and fitted Watson with a bowler. Founded in 1676, Lock has occupied the same premises in St James's since 1765.

The Adventure of the Veiled Lodger, or claret shared with Watson over lunch at "a decent hotel" in *The Adventure of the Cardboard Box*. In *The Adventure of the Abbey Grange* he was able to call upon his knowledge of sediment and of the drawing of a cork—though no wine tasted more delectable to him than the Imperial Tokay he drank at Van Bork's house in *His Last Bow*, from Franz Joseph's special cellar at Vienna's Schönbrunn Palace ("Another glass, Watson?… Might I trouble you to open the window, for chloroform vapor does not help the palate.")

Handily, having picked up his smoking supplies and ammunition, he could have replenished his drinks cellar from **Berry Bros & Rudd** at No. 3, just across the way from the gate tower to Henry VIII's St James's Palace. There has been a shop here since 1698, when a widow named Bourne began selling groceries. A daughter of hers married coffee merchant William Pickering, who

rebuilt both the shop and Stroud Court, behind it, renaming it Pickering Place, in 1734. Approached via a narrow alley, the courtyard is London's smallest public square and was a popular spot for dueling. It was also the location of the legation for the ministers from the Republic of Texas for three years to 1845, at which point "the Lone Star State" threw in its lot with the United States.

From 1765 there was a craze in high society for coming to Berry Bros to be weighed. Among those who tipped the industrial scales were the poet Lord Byron and George "Beau" Brummell, the Regency dandy and friend of the future George IV.

In 1787 an Exeter wine merchant named Berry married into the family, and by 1810 the name Berry had appeared over the shop door, as the business moved into wine, though even today it trades under the sign of the coffee mill. Berry Bros can boast that it supplied wine to the *Titanic*. The "Napoleon Cellar" recalls how the future

OPPOSITE, LEFT:
Shoemakers John Lobb have been in business in St James's since 1866. Their wood-paneled shop has been described by *Esquire* as "the most beautiful in the world." The firm holds Royal Warrants from the Duke of Edinburgh.

OPPOSITE, RIGHT:
Approached by a narrow alley beside the wine merchants Berry Bros & Rudd, London's smallest public square, Pickering Place, was frequently the scene of duels, and until 1845 was home to the legation for ministers for the Republic of Texas.

RIGHT· The Reform Club on Pall Mall was founded in 1836. The palazzo-style building was designed by Charles Barry, architect of the rebuilt Palace of Westminster. Past members have included Sir Arthur Conan Doyle, JM Barrie, HG Wells, and Winston Churchill.

Napoleon III held secret meetings below the shop while in exile.

We turn left now onto **Pall Mall**, home to London's most prestigious gentlemen's clubs, where Mycroft, seven years Sherlock's senior, co-founded and stayed at the Diogenes Club. Perhaps named for Diogenes the cynic, it was begun, said Sherlock, for men who, from shyness or misanthropy, had no wish for company yet were not averse to sinking into an armchair with the day's newspapers. No talking was allowed, on pain of expulsion, except in the Stranger's Room. Arthur Conan Doyle's old club, **the Reform,** at No. 104 was transformed into the Royale

Restaurant for the 2009 movie *Sherlock Holmes*.

One street down from Pall Mall is Carlton House Terrace, where we see the **British Academy,** which appeared as the Diogenes Club in the BBC's *Sherlock*. The Duke of Holdernesse had his London residence on this smart cul-de-sac in *The Adventure of the Priory School,* close, one supposes, to the German Embassy alluded to by Baron Von Herling in *His Last Bow*, when the German spy Von Bork was to "get that signal book through that little door" on the **Duke of York Steps**. The Kaiser's henchman Von Bork was, of course, outwitted by Holmes who, posing as an Irish–American traitor, handed him a package, not of secrets, but a book on bee culture—by one S Holmes.

This broad run of steps leads down from the Duke of York Column, which commemorates Frederick, Duke of York, the second son of George III. If you look up, you'll see a viewing platform. Erected in 1831–3 and topped off with its statue in 1834, the hollow granite tower was for some fifty years accessible to the public, who would pay to ascend the stairs to enjoy a sensational panorama. The metal-studded door has been locked for around 140 years.

At the foot of the steps is the Mall, a great ceremonial avenue with **Buckingham Palace** at the western end. The familiar exterior of this centerpiece of the British monarchy made an appearance in the BBC's *Sherlock*, in the episode "A Scandal in Belgravia". It was to the Palace, in 1902, that Sherlock Holmes might have gone to receive a knighthood, had he not refused it. In that same year, Arthur Conan Doyle accepted one as part of Edward VII's Coronation Honours List— for services rendered in the Boer War. It has been suggested that Irene Adler in *A Scandal in Bohemia* was based on the actress Lily (or Lillie) Langtry, the new king's former mistress and a friend of Conan Doyle's.

The green space opposite the Palace is St James's Park, oldest of London's Royal Parks, where Henry VIII hunted deer, and Holmes and Watson were seen to cross the Blue Bridge in the BBC *Sherlock* episode "The Sign of Three."

BELOW: These artifacts are among the exhibits at the Sherlock Holmes pub (page 64)—including the trademark pipe, matches, and a *Practical Handbook of Bee Culture* that was contained in a packet of supposed state secrets handed to German spy Von Bork.

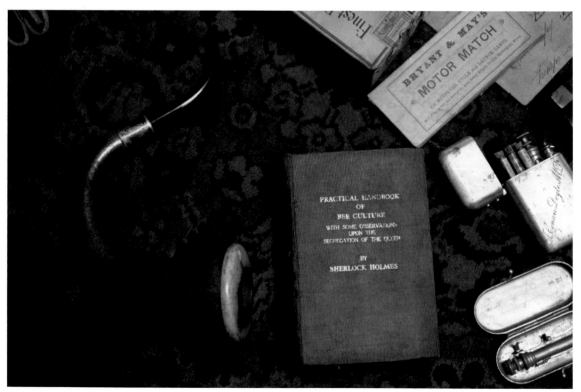

We turn east and pass under the Portland stone Admiralty Arch, designed by Sir Aston Webb. Completed in 1912 and dedicated to Queen Victoria, it was criticized for its vulgarity in mixing triumphal arch with flanking offices, with an apartment above for the Royal Navy top brass. By the time you read this, it may have been reinvented as a five-star hotel.

THE HUB OF A GREAT CITY

So we emerge onto **Trafalgar Square**, the most picture-postcard London cityscape, hub of the metropolis. Here Stapleton hailed John Clayton's hansom cab in *The Hound of the Baskervilles*, claiming to be a detective named Sherlock Holmes and offering the cabbie two guineas to drive him around all day—no questions asked.

The church in the far northeast corner, with a portico supported by six Corinthian columns, is St Martin-in-the-Fields, the parish church for the royal family and for Downing Street. Designed by James Gibbs, it was built in the 1720s. In the days when it looked onto the King's Mews, it was indeed in the fields.

On the north side we see the facade of William Wilkins's **National Gallery**, built on the site of the mews and completed in 1838. Predictably, there were some critical reactions to the building, which William IV dismissed as a "nasty little pokey hole." The gallery was at the center of controversy once more in 1984 when Prince Charles described a proposed extension as "a monstrous carbuncle on the face of a much loved and elegant friend." The Prince had his way; the blue carbuncle was scrapped in favor of a more sympathetic design.

Behind the National Gallery, on St Martin's Place, is the National Portrait Gallery, whose collections include works by Thomas Griffiths Wainewright (1794–1847)—"no mean artist," as Holmes remarked in *The Adventure of the Illustrious Client*. Predictably, though, it was Wainewright the criminal, not Wainewright the artist, who fascinated him. Transported to Tasmania for forging signatures for gain in 1837, Wainewright was suspected of poisoning his uncle, his mother-in-law, and his sister-in-law, who died leaving him money. Doyle spelt the name "Wainwright," but the allusion to TGW is clear. Oscar Wilde wrote that Wainewright was "a forger of no mean or ordinary capabilities, and as a subtle and secret poisoner almost without rival in this or any age."

Fans of the BBC's *Sherlock* will have seen in the episode "The Blind Banker" Watson and Sherlock crossing Trafalgar Square and mounting the National Gallery steps in the shadow of London's most iconic monument. **Nelson's Column** was designed by William Railton, who won the commission by virtue of his "conventional and unexceptional idea of a column surmounted by a statue." (One wonders what the rival competition entrants were like.) It is a Corinthian column of Devon granite. In fact, when Charles Barry was asked to lay out Trafalgar Square, he opposed the erection of Nelson's Column, perceiving that, at nearly 170 feet (51.6m), it would be out of scale and would ruin the effect of the terrace he planned in front of the gallery, to which he added a new wing with seven exhibition rooms and the dome. But the foundations being already dug, the column went up anyway, with the sandstone statue of Lord Nelson, by Edward Hodges Baily, set on top in 1843. Londoners understandably complained that the column was too high for the appreciation of the statue of their hero—even though the 5 foot 6 inch (1.7m) tall admiral stands here 17 feet (5.2m) tall and weighs 16 tons.

The column is guarded by Sir Edwin Landseer's four bronze lions. Landseer was a favorite with Victorians—his *Monarch of the Glen* stag graces many a shortbread tin—but he had never before sculpted. In 1868, a quarter of a century after the completion of the monument, the lions finally arrived, to the usual howls of derision. One distinguished animal painter pronounced that the beasts "must be quietly damned because… they miss the true sculptural

NELSON'S COLUMN TRAFALGAR DAY. 4633.
(1897)

L.S.& P.Cº

quality which distinguishes the leonine pose."
Four years later, Landseer was certified insane.
Upon his death in 1873 crowds flocked to the
square, and his lions were draped with wreaths.
Today's tourists, not really bothered about
whether the leonine pose is lifelike, just love to
clamber on a lion and sit atop the lion's mane.

The fountains in the square were designed by the
architect Sir Edwin Lutyens in the late 1930s and
came into use in 1948. Charles Barry's original
quatrefoil fountains, dating from 1845, are what
Doyle would have known but are now in Canada.

The bronze equestrian statue of Charles I, cast
in 1633 by the French sculptor Hubert Le Sueur,
gazes down Whitehall toward the site of the king's
beheading, outside Inigo Jones's Banqueting
House, in 1649. After the Civil War the statue was
sold to a metalworker named John Rivett, to be
broken down. With great business acumen, Rivett
instead hid (perhaps buried) the statue, producing
some odds and ends of brass as "proof" of its
destruction, and ran a nice line in metal-handled
knives and forks that he claimed were made from
the statue remains. Upon the Restoration of the
monarchy, it was discovered by the Earl of
Portland, bought by Charles II, and erected here
in 1675.

SEAT OF GOVERNMENT

Whitehall, you will recall, was where brother
Mycroft worked, shuttling like a tram on rails
between his offices and the Diogenes Club. It was
his job, occasionally, to audit the books for various
government departments, though in truth he *was*
the Government, Sherlock confided—he was a
specialist in omniscience. "Again and again his
word has decided the national policy," he said in
The Adventure of the Bruce-Partington Plans.

OPPOSITE: The very hub of London, Trafalgar Square, on
Trafalgar Day, 1897. Nelson's Column towers over all, topped with the
16-ton statue of Admiral Lord Nelson. Behind is the National Gallery
and, in the northeast corner, St Martin-in-the-Fields.

On the left we find Great Scotland Yard (page
65) and Whitehall Place. 3 Whitehall Place is the
billet of the Department of Energy and Climate
Change and is where, in the BBC's *Sherlock*,
Holmes stood upon the rooftop. 4 Whitehall Place
was the original home of the Metropolitan Police
from 1829 till 1890, with its back entrance on
Great Scotland Yard. Here worked the inimitable
Lestrade, "the pick of a bad lot" (along with
Gregson) in Holmes's estimation (in *A Study in
Scarlet*)—"a little, sallow, rat-faced, dark-eyed
fellow" and "a lean, ferret-like man" in Watson's
accounting (in *A Study in Scarlet* and *The Boscombe
Valley Mystery* respectively). Lestrade was in the
habit of dropping in at Baker Street in the
evenings, enabling Holmes to keep in touch with
all that went on at HQ. They did not put too
much stress upon security, we gather.

On the right, in front of the **Admiralty**
complex, stands a 140-foot (72.7m) colonnaded
screen wall designed by Robert Adam in 1759,
with flanking pavilions and a central arch with
seahorse decorations. Behind the Admiralty
Screen, at the left of the complex, is a 1720s
brick building with stone dressing. Previously
known as The Admiralty, it is now called the Old
Admiralty (or the Ripley Building, as it was
designed by Thomas Ripley). This is where Lord
Nelson's body lay overnight before his funeral,
and it contains the Admiralty Board Room.
Adjoining this building are the late 18th-century
Admiralty House in yellow brick and the larger,
late 19th-century Admiralty Extension in red
brick with stone dressings. As the official
residence of the First Lord of the Admiralty until
1964, Admiralty House was home to both the
Duke of Holdernesse in *The Adventure of the Priory
School*, and to Winston Churchill for two stints, in
1911–15 and 1939–40.

The Admiralty was "buzzing like an overturned
beehive" upon the theft of the Bruce-Partington
Plans. It was also the source of a government cover-
up, when the transport ship *Gloria Scott* was "set
down by the Admiralty as being lost at sea, and no

word has ever leaked out as to her true fate" (except, that is, in *The Memoirs of Sherlock Holmes*).

Next on the right, beyond the Admiralty complex, we find **Downing Street,** the site of the official residences of the Prime Minister (No. 10) and the Chancellor (No. 11). In *The Adventure of the Naval Treaty* Sherlock sent his card up to Lord Holdhurst in his Downing Street chambers and "was instantly shown up."

At the end of Whitehall, looking left along the Victoria Embankment, we see the **Norman**

Shaw Buildings. In 1890, they became New Scotland Yard—and, in 1967, the *old* New Scotland Yard, when the police force moved its HQ again. One of this pair of redbrick buildings, by Richard Norman Shaw, took custody of some macabre exhibits. The Scotland Yard Crime Museum, begun in 1874, comprises a collection of nooses, criminals' death masks, weaponry, and such curiosities as the Jack the Ripper "From Hell" letter (page 49), along with the possessions of hanged murderer Charles Peace (pages 49 and 75), including his single-string violin and his last bow. The museum is not open to the public. It was set up for "instructional purposes" for serving officers—who would on occasion faint in horror—but privileged individuals could visit by invitation. Among those to do so were Laurel and Hardy, Gilbert and Sullivan, the escapologist Harry Houdini, Sir Arthur Conan Doyle, and—count on it!—Sherlock Holmes. The famous air gun fashioned by the blind German mechanic Von Herder to the order of Professor Moriarty would, he hazarded in *The Adventure of the Empty House*, embellish the collection.

Doyle gained an entrée in December 1892, taking along the writer Jerome K Jerome and his future brother-in-law Willie Hornung, who was

OPPOSITE: The Old Admiralty Building was headed by the First Lord of the Admiralty on the eve of World War I, when the German spy Von Bork complained that the Admiralty had changed all the naval codes. It was to be the least of his worries.

RIGHT: The entrance to New Scotland Yard, the Metropolitan Police headquarters from 1890 till 1967. It has been known as the Norman Shaw Building, after its architect. It is home to the police Crime Museum, a collection of macabre exhibits, not open to the public.

then engaged to Arthur's sister Connie. Did the museum give Hornung ideas? He went on, in 1898, to create the gentleman thief Raffles and his sidekick, Bunny Manders, "a kind of inversion" of Holmes and Watson, as Doyle saw it. He did not approve of stories that glamorized the crooked man, explaining, "I confess I think they are dangerous. You must not make the criminal a hero."

The iron and granite **Westminster Bridge**, upon which the poet William Wordsworth stood in awe in 1802, is painted green to reflect the color of the leather seats of the House of Commons in the adjacent Palace of Westminster. Lambeth Bridge, upriver, is painted red, the color of the seating in the House of Lords. Over Westminster Bridge went Holmes and Watson at a smart clip in *The Disappearance of Lady Frances Carfax,* passing the Houses of Parliament as a glance at the clock tower of Big Ben told them it was twenty-five to eight.

From the bridge, one sees (as Wordsworth could not have done) that emblematic tower known to all by the name of its great bell, Big Ben, and the **Palace of Westminster**. Designed in the Perpendicular Gothic style, it is the work of Sir Charles Barry, and of "God's own architect," the brilliant, driven Augustus Welby Pugin. Neither man would live to see the building's completion in 1870. "Big Ben" was one of Pugin's last designs before his death in 1852 at the age of 40, insane and probably syphilitic. Charles Barry died in 1860. In the 2009 movie *Sherlock Holmes*, Lord Blackwood, having taken control of the Temple of the Four Orders, proceeded with his plan to overthrow the government here. Not a chance!

RIGHT: Time lord. The clock tower popularly known as Big Ben has been counting off the seconds since 1859. Tours are available only to UK residents, who can climb the 334 spiral steps, go behind the clock faces, and hear the great sonorous bell strike the hour.

INVESTIGATIONS BY THE YARD

Crime detection in the London of Sherlock Holmes

*"They say that genius is an infinite capacity for taking pains.
It's a very bad definition, but it does apply to detective work."*

Sherlock Holmes, *A Study in Scarlet*

In the slums of Whitechapel, east London, over barely six weeks in 1888, five women of the night were murdered and mutilated by the elusive psychopath known as "Leather Apron" and, more enduringly, "Jack the Ripper." The Whitechapel Murders were so horrific that they riveted the popular imagination, and Scotland Yard, with the City Police, was under intense pressure to capture the killer—but how?

At a time of dazzling advances in other fields, police investigation was still plodding along, heavily dependent on the bloodied knife, the smoking gun, eye-witness testimony, and confessions. The science underpinning detection was sketchy, at times not scientific at all, leading to incalculable miscarriages of justice.

Professional investigators recognized the value of crime-scene examination, where the position of a body, blood, wheel tracks, and shoe prints could all tell a tale. They were waking up to the dangers of contaminating the scene, but too often spectators were able to trample and handle vital evidence. Crime-scene photography was not routine. All the Ripper's victims were photographed in the mortuary but, while officers made sketches of the crime scene, in the case of only one of the victims, Mary Jane Kelly, was it photographed.

Serology, blood analysis, was in its infancy. There was no reliable test to distinguish a bloodstain from a rust or fruit stain. Murder trials depended on the *opinion* of a doctor or policeman that smears, spots, spatters were indeed blood. Not until 1901 was a test developed to distinguish human from animal blood, and the ABO human blood groups were delineated.

WHAT'S YOUR POISON?

Postmortem examinations of murder victims were performed without delay, since cadavers could not be refrigerated. There were tests to detect arsenic, chloroform, and certain vegetable poisons in human tissue, but toxicology was not well advanced. For this reason, and because lethal substances were so readily obtainable, poisoning was common (page 47).

Heaven knows, we have Holmes himself shooting cocaine with impunity (he was a "self-poisoner" in the words of the disapproving Watson); his bedroom

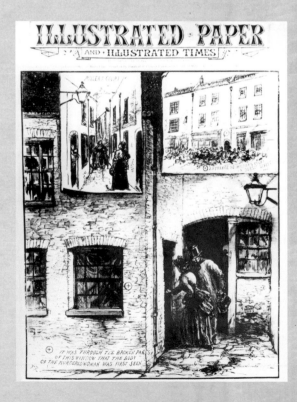

RIGHT: Appealing to salacious public appetites, a tabloid paper reports how the mutilated body of Jack the Ripper's victim Mary Kelly was seen through a broken window in her room in Miller Court, by her landlord's young assistant.

mantelpiece was littered with syringes. Opium was similarly legal. When Watson took a cab to fetch Holmes from the Bar of Gold opium den in *The Man with the Twisted Lip*, Holmes assured him that he had not "added opium-smoking to cocaine injections, and all the other little weaknesses on which you have favored me with your medical views."

Watson, meanwhile, with his doctor's hat on, could prescribe strychnine as a sedative. Druggists sold Hall's Coca Wine (liquid cocaine) as a tonic, while Bayer's Heroin tablets soothed a cough. Overdose was a real and present danger. The line between medicine and poison is blurred. All drugs are toxic at some level— "the dose makes the poison," as Paracelsus said.

Implicated in a third of all deliberate poisonings of the 19th century, arsenic was everywhere in late Victorian England. The very walls exuded it; fashionable green wallpapers were colored with Scheele's Green pigment containing it, causing illness and fatalities, notably among children. William Morris, leading light of the Arts and Crafts movement (and wallpaper producer), dismissed concerns over the deadly decor as a great folly, writing in a letter in 1885 that "the doctors were bitten by witch fever."

Arsenic was an ingredient of cosmetics, and, with strychnine, of common household cleaning products; it might freely be put down as rat poison. Accidental and self-poisoning were a daily hazard.

HOUNDING THE RIPPER

Police dogs had been used in continental Europe from around 1860, when fierce breeds served as bodyguards, as deterrents, and for crowd control. But over the next 20 years the possibility began to open up of training them for "nose work." Two bloodhounds, Burgho and Barnaby, were drafted in with a view to getting them to sniff out Jack the Ripper. They were set tracking tests by the Metropolitan Police Commissioner, Sir Charles Warren, in the Royal Parks, and acquitted themselves well, but the press mocked, their readers scorned, and the dogs were sent home with their tails between their legs.

RIGHT: Drawings show bloodhounds Burgho and Barnaby set to track Police Commissioner Sir Charles Warren across Hyde Park as a trial. By the time of Mary Kelly's murder (opposite), the sniffer dogs had been reclaimed by their owner.

A CASE OF IDENTITY

Percy Lefroy Mapleton has the dubious distinction of having been the subject of the first police "wanted" picture to appear in the national press. His composite portrait was based on descriptions of him and published in the *Daily Telegraph*. Mapleton had murdered and robbed a fellow passenger on a Brighton-bound train in June 1881. He was discovered hiding in Stepney, east London, his bloodied clothing still in the room, having pawned his revolver. He was hanged in November 1881 and found fame briefly as a waxwork in Madame Tussaud's Chamber of Horrors. The officer in charge of the case? One Detective Inspector Holmes (no relation).

With no witnesses, no description, no idea whatsoever of the Ripper's identity, such a composite portrait was not possible. It was left to the *Illustrated Police News*—a salacious rag pandering to public prurience—to publish two drawings in October 1888, but they represented nothing more enlightening than an artist's idea of how such a fiend *might* look.

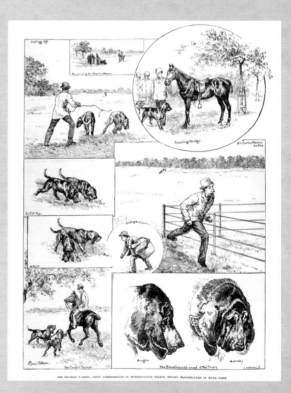

FOOT FOLLOWERS

Criminals must stand somewhere, somehow; they must enter and leave the crime scene—in brogues or ballet pumps, or barefoot. Shoes wear in different places. Match a shoe to a print and you are getting somewhere. One's tread leaves deposits of soil, sand, clay, carpet fluff. Footprints were used by the Victorian police to infer height (length of stride), gender, type of occupation, social status, and much more. Hand prints, also, were examined in terms of size and peculiarities. The science of fingerprinting, however, was only then emerging. A Scottish physician, Henry Faulds, proposed study of "the skin-furrows of the hand" to Scotland Yard in 1888 and was rejected. In 1892, Sir Francis Galton published *Finger Prints*, in which he identified the arches, loops, whorls, and pockets that characterized fingerprint patterns. But "dactyloscopy," as the science of fingerprinting became known, was only finally introduced in Britain after the turn of the century.

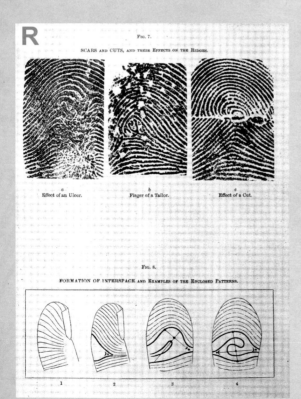

FIG. 7.

SCARS AND CUTS, AND THEIR EFFECTS ON THE RIDGES.

a
Effect of an Ulcer.

b
Finger of a Tailor.

c
Effect of a Cut.

FIG. 8.

FORMATION OF INTERSPACE AND EXAMPLES OF THE ENCLOSED PATTERNS.

1   2   3   4

MEASURE FOR MEASURE

While the police remained skeptical of fingerprinting, they bought enthusiastically into a system known as "bertillonage," developed by Alphonse Bertillon, "the father of scientific detection," in 1879. A clerk based at the police department in Paris, Bertillon introduced "mug shots" (portrait photographs, full face and in profile, in standard lighting conditions) and devised techniques of document examination, the use of galvanoplastic compounds to preserve footprints, and a "dynamometer" to establish the degree of force used to break and enter.

Concerned by the levels of recidivism in France, he contrived a means to identify career criminals, designing gauges and calipers to measure those features that remain constant in adulthood (one sees a novel use for the hatter's conformateur mentioned on page 35!), averring that there was just a one-in-286-million chance of two individuals having precisely the same Bertillon scores. Bertillonage included body measurements, photographs, a *portrait parlé* (verbal description), and, somewhat to Bertillon's reluctance, fingerprints. "Thanks to a French genius," proclaimed the patriotic national press, "errors of identification will soon cease to exist… judicial errors based on false identification will likewise disappear… *Vive* Bertillon!"

Bertillonage was, however, only applicable to serial criminals—known suspects who had previously been arrested, photographed, measured. It relied upon the absolute accuracy by which measurements were taken and recorded, and it was vulnerable to human error and noncompliant prisoners.

Back in October 1878, police in Blackheath, southeast London, had picked up the most noncompliant prisoner of them all, an armed cat burglar who had shot at one of them. The strange, "thin and slightly built" man with the twisted lip refused to give his name. He was described to Greenwich Police Court as being about 60 years of age and "of repellent aspect." Had the practice of branding prisoners not been abandoned, they would have known he had previous convictions. Had

LEFT: In his book *Finger Prints*, published in 1892, Sir Francis Galton reasoned that the print patterns were unique to the individual. But it was Henry Faulds who first proposed it, in an academic paper published in the journal *Nature* in 1880. Was he robbed?

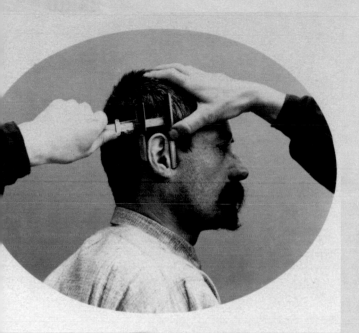

ABOVE: Alphonse Bertillon's method of identification entailed the use of specially designed gauges to take minute measurements. It was his belief that there was but a one-in-286-million chance of two individuals having identical Bertillon scores.

bertillonage been already in use, they might have quickly realized that this peculiar character was none other than the most-wanted murderer Charles Peace, aged 44, the human chameleon whom we shall meet on page 75. He could have been banged to rights!

Scars, birthmarks, and tattoos could similarly assist in identification. But with no computer search engines in those days, if the criminal was Mr Average then bertillonage would have entailed endless paperwork in the quest to find the perfect match. Of course, the same must also have been true of matching up fingerprints, but it was fingerprinting that would eventually win the day.

PEN TO PAPER

Amid the panic surrounding the Whitechapel atrocities, police and press received hundreds of hoax communications purportedly from the killer. Possibly two—the "From Hell" and "Dear Boss" letters—were genuine. So did the investigators miss a trick? Five years later, on being shown the "From Hell" letter on

ABOVE: Among a slew of missives claiming to be from Jack the Ripper, the barely literate "From Hell" letter was believed to be genuine. It was sent to George Lusk, head of the Whitechapel Vigilance Committee, enclosing a piece of a kidney (since lost).

his visit to the Scotland Yard Crime Museum (page 42), Doyle expressed surprise that the police had failed to do what Sherlock Holmes would have done—that is, to copy it and publish it in the newspapers in the hope that someone could come up with a match for it.

What they had done instead was to turn to handwriting "experts." The analysis of handwriting may be a useful tool, especially where forgery is suspected, but although it was admissible as evidence, it was an inexact science that led to more than one wrongful conviction.

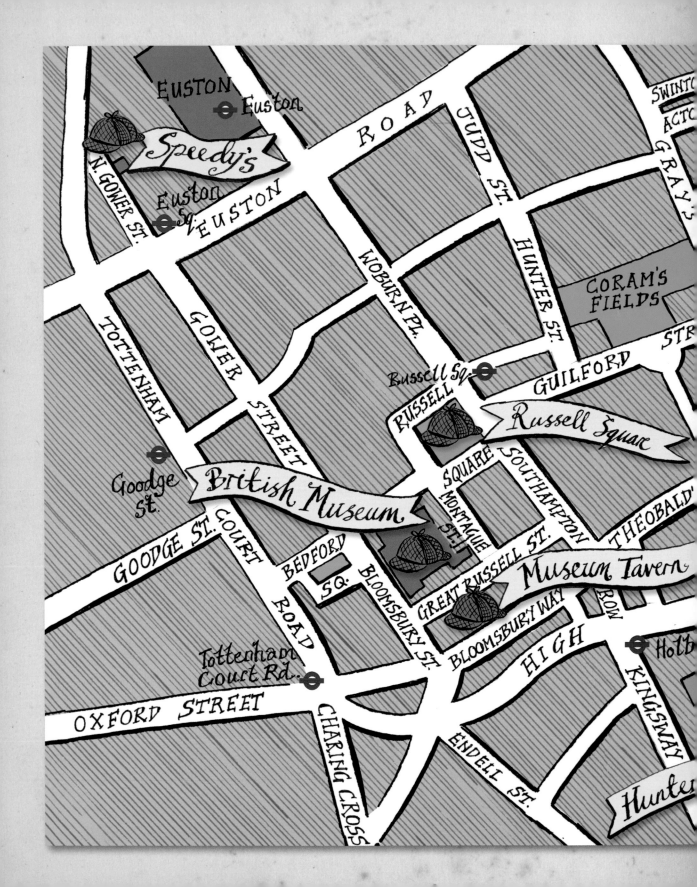

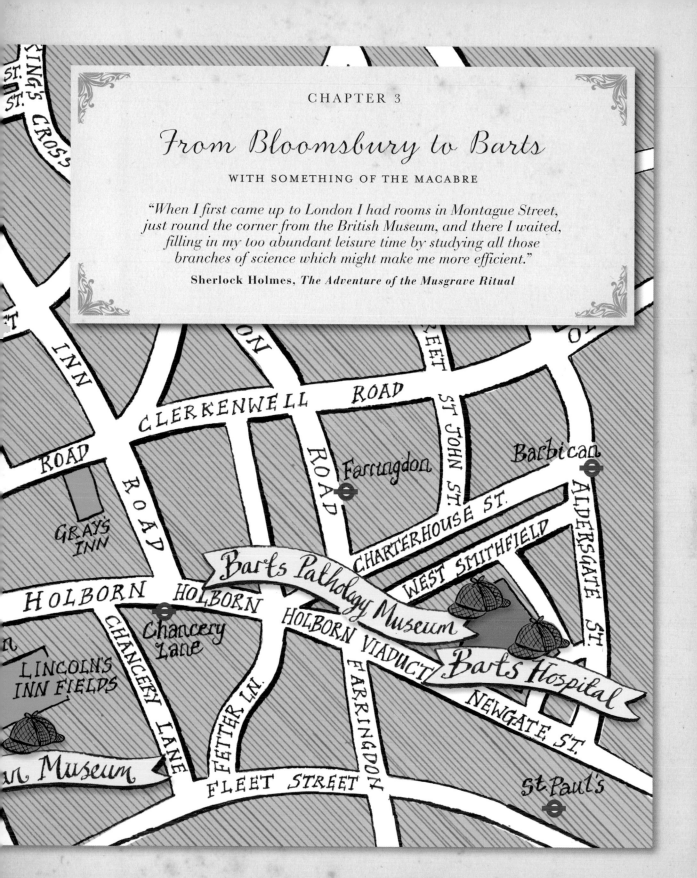

CHAPTER 3

From Bloomsbury to Barts

WITH SOMETHING OF THE MACABRE

*"When I first came up to London I had rooms in Montague Street,
just round the corner from the British Museum, and there I waited,
filling in my too abundant leisure time by studying all those
branches of science which might make me more efficient."*

Sherlock Holmes, *The Adventure of the Musgrave Ritual*

Sherlock Holmes had on his doorstep, in those early days in London, the foremost resource for his studies. The circular, domed reading room at the **British Museum** on Great Russell Street—its design inspired by the Pantheon in Rome—was open to "the world at large," at no charge. Prospective users had to apply in writing, be at least 21, use it purely for "a literary purpose such as study, reference or research," and be possessed of "respectability."

As he checked out Stapleton's credentials in *The Hound of the Baskervilles* and pored over Eckermann's tract on voodoo worship in *The Adventure of Wisteria Lodge*, Holmes could have found himself sitting alongside a bearded Karl Marx as he worked on the last volume of *Das Kapital*, Vladimir Lenin, Bram Stoker, creator of *Dracula*, Oscar Wilde, and—well, why not?—the mustachioed Sir Arthur Conan Doyle.

The brainchild of Antonio Panizzi, the Keeper of Printed Books, and designed by Sydney Smirke, the Reading Room opened in 1857; 140 years later, the wealth of books were moved to a new home in St Pancras and the Reading Room was then restored. Today it is an exhibition space.

You could lose yourself all day in the museum, admiring the Parthenon Frieze, the Rosetta Stone, the Mummy of Katebet, the Great Agra Treasure… But if you work up a thirst, on a corner just across from the south front in Great Russell Street—its colonnade and pediment

OPPOSITE: An all-round education—the British Museum's circular Reading Room opened its doors in 1857, to anyone, on application. Users had to be "respectable"; Karl Marx forfeited his right of entry after he pawned his overcoat.

RIGHT: 221B or not 221B? Martin Freeman as Watson outside the famous Baker Street address—in reality on North Gower Street—in the BBC's *Sherlock*. Behind him is Speedy's café, a hugely popular location, which appeared in the pilot episode as Mrs Hudson's Snax.

recalling classical Greece, with statues representing the Progress of Civilization—stands the **Museum Tavern**. Formerly the Dog and Duck, it began life in the 18th century, but what we see is solidly Victorian, the work of the architect William Finch Hill. Marx and Doyle, taking time out for a beer, would have glimpsed themselves in the same gilt-framed mirrors, admired the same carved wood fittings. The pub is prime contender for the Alpha Inn frequented by Henry Baker in *The Adventure of the Blue Carbuncle*. Welcoming to visitors without being touristy, it serves real ales, world beers, a good choice of wines, and hearty food (fish and chips, pies, roasts).

Fans of the BBC's *Sherlock* might prefer to give antiquities a miss and begin the day instead north of the museum, with a cappuccino or full English breakfast at **Speedy's Sandwich Bar & Café** (187 North Gower Street). You can buy a souvenir mug or T-shirt before crossing Euston Road and heading down Gower Street—on which Charles Darwin rented a house (No. 110) while working on his theory of natural selection.

For the writer Ford Madox Ford, who went to school on Gower Street, Bloomsbury was a place of "dismal, decorous, unhappy, glamorous squares"—but he grew up among the "tumultuous bearded and moral great" of the late Victorian era and had an axe to grind. On a summer's day, **Russell Square**, off Montague Place, will strike the visitor as anything but gloomy. It was at a boarding house on the square that Hilton Cubitt met and fell "as much in love as a man can be" with Elsie Patrick in *The Adventure of the Dancing Men*. Here, too, Mike Stamford introduced Dr

Watson to Benedict Cumberbatch's Sherlock.

Pause to admire Sir Richard Westmacott's 1809 statue of Francis Russell, 5th Duke of Bedford, and the terra-cotta-clad Hotel Russell. Built in 1898, it was designed by Charles Fitzroy Doll and based on the 16th-century Château de Madrid that used to be on the edge of the Bois de Boulogne in Paris. The hotel is adorned with life-size statues of British queens, by Henry Charles Fehr.

On the western corner of the square there is a green-painted wooden hut, somewhat reminiscent of a garden shed. This is one of 13 survivors of 60 or so shelters built in London after 1875, to offer a hot meal and a drink (no alcohol) to the drivers of hansom cabs and, later, hackney carriages. Newspapers were provided, gambling

and foul language forbidden. The shelters, according to a contemporary account, "are the cabman's restaurants, and the cabman, as a rule, is not so much a large drinker as a large eater. At one shelter lately the great feature was boiled rabbit and pickled pork at two o'clock in the morning, and for two weeks a small warren of Ostenders [rabbits packed in a certain way] was consumed nightly." The shelters are more spacious than they appear from the outside. A dozen or so cabbies can squeeze inside. On warm days they sit out eating bacon sandwiches—though not boiled rabbit—alfresco.

From Russell Square, head south on Southampton Row, crossing High Holborn to Kingsway. (Gone, now, is the opulent Holborn Restaurant that once stood on the corner, with its marbled King's Hall and three galleries, where Watson took young Stamford to lunch on turtle soup and lamb cutlets or some such, in *A Study in Scarlet*.)

East of Kingsway, just behind the Royal Courts of Justice, is **Lincoln's Inn Fields**, where at lunchtime office workers eat their sushi and sandwiches under giant London plane trees. The city's largest public square, it was laid out in the 1630s, in part to designs by Inigo Jones. A handsome building on the west side, known as Lindsey House, was built in around 1640, possibly to designs by Inigo Jones, making it a rare survivor from the Civil War period, when Oliver Cromwell ruled Britain, as a king in all but name.

With the Restoration of the monarchy, Cromwell's successor, Charles II—"The Merry Monarch"—had many mistresses. One of them, the actress "pretty, witty" Nell Gwynne, had

lodgings at Lincoln's Inn Fields when she was performing in a theater nearby.

On the south side of Lincoln's Inn Fields is the Royal College of Surgeons. Its museums were rebuilt in 1834–7 and 1851–2 under the direction of Charles Barry, but today, only the library and portico remain of the 19th-century building, following bomb damage in World War II, after which the museums were once again rebuilt. Dr Watson, as an army surgeon, was surely a member or fellow of the college.

For the general public, the RCS has one extraordinary resource, the **Hunterian Museum**. Though there is no record of Holmes visiting the Hunterian, he could not have stayed away. The museum had its beginnings with John Hunter (1728–93), a keen student of anatomy, a surgeon, and a dab hand with a dissecting scalpel, whose collection of some 13,000 animal and human specimens was bought by the nation after his death, forming the basis of the museum.

An 1870s account of the exhibits reads, "Among the objects of curiosity preserved here are the skeletons of several human beings and animals, which during the time of their existence had obtained some celebrity. Among them may be mentioned… Mlle Crachani, a Sicilian dwarf, who at the age of ten years was just twenty inches [51cm] high, Charles Byrne, or O'Brien, the Irish giant, who at his death measured eight feet four inches [2.5m], and also the gigantic elephant 'Chunee,' which was formerly exhibited on the stage at Covent Garden Theatre." Alas, poor Chunee!

Hunterian Museum

A place, in the Victorian era, of bones and bell jars, like some great knacker's yard or charnel house, the Hunterian has been described as "a postmortem palace." The bomb damage it suffered in World War II resulted in the loss of two-thirds of its collections. Today it is presented as a Crystal Gallery, with everything behind glass, but there is much to fascinate, from a cancerous warthog skull to Sir Winston Churchill's dentures, from a false nose for a syphilitic woman to Sir Isaac Newton's death mask, from the skeleton of Jonathan Wild, hanged at Tyburn in 1725, to that of a dodo. Only be warned—some exhibits are truly shocking, affecting, or toe-curling. A gallery tracing the development of surgical instruments boggles the imagination.

OPPOSITE: One of the 13 surviving cabmen's shelters in London. Relocated from pedestrianized Leicester Square, this one is on Russell Square and is still much used by hungry taxi drivers. It was a gift from actor-manager Squire Bancroft. The rules forbade all gambling, card games, and foul language in the shelters.

ABOVE: Hunter gatherer. The often weird, sometimes macabre, specimens collected by surgeon John Hunter formed the basis of the Hunterian Museum at the Royal College of Surgeons. It is no longer quite the knacker's yard it appears here.

Just east of Lincoln's Inn Fields is Lincoln's Inn, the earliest of London's four Inns of Court, to which all barristers belong. Lincoln's Inn traces its history back to 1422, its origins lost in the mists of time. The Tudor redbrick appearance is not misleading—the Old Hall dates from 1489. On weekdays visitors can wander the precincts, and group guided tours are available by arrangement.

The monumental entrance to Lincoln's Inn on the east side opens onto Chancery Lane. North is High Holborn, from where, via Holborn Viaduct, one can walk to West Smithfield and **St Bartholomew's Hospital**. It was in a wing at "Barts," in an upstairs lab, that Holmes confounded Watson, a stranger, with a firm handshake and an affable, "How are you? You have been in Afghanistan, I perceive." (*A Study in Scarlet*)

Originally founded in 1123, by a courtier of Henry I, as a hospital and priory where the sick and destitute of Smithfield were tended by the monks and nuns, Barts fell on hard times when the priory was closed by Henry VIII as part of the dissolution of the monasteries, in 1539. Henry was persuaded to re-found the hospital in 1546, and granted it to the City of London. The capital's only public statue of that megalomaniac monarch, dating from 1702, stands above the Henry VIII Gate on Giltspur Street.

In 1729–70 the hospital was rebuilt to the designs of James Gibbs, who was also the architect of St Martin-in-the Fields on Trafalgar Square. In the 1730s, William Hogarth adorned the grand staircase with depictions of the parable of The Good Samaritan, and Christ at the Pool of Bethesda, exalting the spirit of the hospital's work. The tower of the Church of St Bartholomew the

Less survives from the Middle Ages.

To visit St Bartholomew's Pathology Museum—one of the world's ten weirdest medical museums, in the judgment of CNN—enter the complex through the Henry VIII Gate, on Giltspur Street. The collection comprises more than five thousand medical specimens, housed over three levels of the Victorian museum building. Exhibits range from the bound foot of a Chinese woman to the damaged liver of a straitlaced lady, from an engineer's thumb to "chimney sweep's cancer," from a devil's foot to the skull of John Bellingham, hanged for the murder of the British Prime Minister Spencer Perceval, whom he shot through the heart in 1812.

Built in 1879, the museum would have been at Holmes's disposal in pursuit of his outré researches. It is claimed that Arthur Conan Doyle wrote some of the short stories in what is now the office of the technical curator.

After Holmes plunged from the hospital roof in the episode "A Study in Pink" of the BBC's *Sherlock*, the telephone box by the Henry VIII Gate was plastered with messages from distraught well-wishers praying for his safety.

They should have known he would bounce back. There are few certainties in this life, but The Return of Sherlock Holmes is one of them.

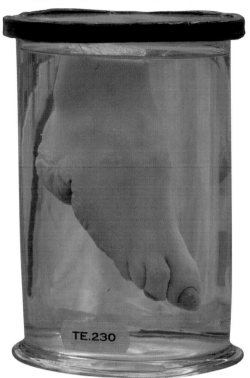

TE.230

OPPOSITE: The swinging detective. Fans of the BBC's *Sherlock* watched in horror as our hero appeared to plunge to his doom from the roof of Bart's Hospital. "Suicide of fake genius," screamed a headline in the *Sun* newspaper. "Gotcha!" Holmes might have replied, echoing the paper's notorious Falklands War headline.

ABOVE RIGHT: The bound foot of a Chinese woman among specimens in Bart's pathology museum. Begun in infancy, the creation of a "lotus foot" entailed the breaking of the arch of the foot and every toe except the big one.

RIGHT: The skull of John Bellingham, sentenced to be hanged, dissected, and anatomized for the murder in 1812 of Prime Minister Spencer Perceval. Bellingham had described his action as "a warning to all future ministers… that they will henceforth do the thing that is right." Ho, ho!

A MAVERICK AT WORK

The forensic science of Sherlock Holmes

"I've found it! I've found it... a reagent which is precipitated by hemoglobin, and by nothing else... it gives us an infallible test for blood stains."

Sherlock Holmes, *A Study in Scarlet*

So Sherlock Holmes greeted his visitors when young Stamford first took Dr Watson to meet his prospective fellow lodger in *A Study in Scarlet*. Holmes was, Stamford warned, "a little queer in his ideas," a bit cold-blooded. Stamford could imagine him slipping a friend an experimental pinch of the latest vegetable alkaloid poison—or, to be fair, taking it himself. The pair found Holmes at Barts, in "a lofty chamber lined and littered with countless bottles," elated by the discovery of a test to distinguish bloodstains.

The man was relentless in the pursuit of truth, honing his art with test tube and retort. He interested himself in ballistics and would try the tolerance of his landlady, Mrs Hudson—not to mention Watson's—by firing off bullets in the apartment to study their trajectory, sitting in his armchair picking out a patriotic "VR" in bullet pocks, improving neither the atmosphere nor the appearance of the room.

In pursuit of "out-of-the-way knowledge," he might be found in the dissecting room at Barts, beating corpses with a stick to see how they bruised. He was an amateur, self-taught maverick, yet in many of his methods he was years, even decades, ahead of established police practice.

Such was his pioneering influence that he appears on timelines of forensic science along with the likes of Mathieu Orfila, "the father of toxicology," and Sir Alec Jeffreys, "the father of DNA evidence."

Examples include such entries as the following, all for 1887:

"Arthur Conan Doyle publishes his first Sherlock Holmes story."

"In... *A Study in Scarlet*, Holmes develops a chemical to determine whether a stain was blood or not—something that had not yet been done in a real-life investigation."

"Arthur Conan Doyle published the first Sherlock

" HOLMES WAS WORKING HARD OVER A CHEMICAL INVESTIGATION."

Holmes story in Beeton's Christmas Annual of London 1887."

Holmes was acutely alive to the importance of protecting a crime scene. ("Just sit in the corner there, Watson, that your footprints may not complicate matters."—*The Sign of Four*) Though his test for blood was fiction, it prefigured discoveries made 14 and more years later.

Among his various monographs was one on the art of tracing footsteps, "with some remarks upon the use of plaster of Paris as a preserver of impresses," for, he said, there was no branch of detective science so important or so neglected. A peg leg, a pygmy, running feet, walking feet, a ribbed tennis shoe… time and again, footprints helped to lead Sherlock Holmes to his quarry. So, too, the tracks of bicycle tires: "I am familiar with forty-two different impressions left by tires," he advised Watson in *The Adventure of the Priory School*. "This, as you perceive, is a Dunlop, with a patch upon the outer cover. Heidegger's tires were Palmer's, leaving longitudinal stripes."

While he could not so overstep the mark as to perform postmortem examinations, he employed toxicology based on observation. ("I dabble with poisons a great deal," he said in *A Study in Scarlet*.) Devil's-foot root, charcoal, opium, a variant of strychnine, and an alkaloid extract from a South American arrow all figured in his inquiries.

Whereas nothing but derision had come out of the Burgho-and-Barnaby snarl-up in the hunt for Jack the Ripper (page 47), Holmes made good use of sniffer dogs. In *The Sign of Four* he borrowed Toby, the bird-stuffer's mutt: "a queer mongrel, with a most amazing power of scent. I would rather have Toby's

OPPOSITE: Dabbling in poisons? In *A Study in Scarlet* young Stamford remarked that it would not be beyond Sherlock Holmes to slip a friend vegetable alkaloid to discover its effects. Poisoning was a favorite murder method in the Victorian age when toxicology was not well advanced.

BELOW: Body of evidence. A dissecting room c.1900. With forensic science not highly developed, investigation of the Whitechapel murders depended on examination of the victims' bodies and the letters sent to investigators.

help than that of the whole detective force in London." And in *The Adventure of the Missing Three-Quarter* it was Pompey, "pride of the local draghounds," who followed the scent of aniseed to find Godfrey Staunton.

When it came to handwriting, in *The Adventure of the Reigate Squire*, Holmes swiftly discerned that the words on a scrap of paper in the murder victim's hand had been written alternately by two related people, one young, one old. ("When I draw your attention to the strong t's of 'at' and 'to' and ask you to compare them with the weak ones of 'quarter' and 'twelve,' you will instantly recognize the fact.") In *The Adventure of the Norwood Builder* he deduced that a document supposed to be the will of Jonas Oldacre was a fake. "This was written on a train. The good writing represents stations, the bad writing movement, and the very bad writing passing over points."

But he did not stop there, for he produced a monograph, *The Typewriter and its Relation to Crime*. In *A Case of Identity*, in 1891, he observed, "It is a

curious thing that a typewriter has really quite as much individuality as a man's handwriting."

Typewriters were a relatively recent import from America. Gun-makers Remington had launched the first commercial typewriter with its QWERTY keyboard in 1873, but it had failed to catch on until the marketing targeted women. In *A Case of Identity*, Holmes's client Mary Sutherland, earning two pennies a sheet at her keyboard, was one of an emerging breed of "typewriter girls." Holmes's perspicacity is the more remarkable for that. In a rare instance of product placement, Laura Lyons was found seated before a Remington in *The Hound of the Baskervilles*.

One method we never find Holmes using is bertillonage (page 48). Though he expressed enthusiastic admiration for "that French savant" and his system of measurements, there may have been an element of professional jealousy. In *The Hound of the Baskervilles* he became prickly at Dr Mortimer's suggestion that he, Holmes, was but the second-highest expert in Europe. "Indeed, Sir! May I enquire who has the honor to be the first?" he asked with asperity—and, on hearing the name Bertillon, he huffed, "Then had you not better consult him?"

But the fact remained that bertillonage had very little application at a crime scene. Even the great Sherlock Holmes could not have been expected to intuit the width of a suspect's right ear or the length of his left middle finger.

Stung by Mortimer's words, Holmes would have been gratified to know that, in Egypt at any rate, there was no question as to who was the highest authority in Europe. On a stay in Cairo, Arthur Conan Doyle found that his Sherlock Holmes stories had been translated into Arabic by order of the Khedive and were in use as police textbooks. Hong Kong followed suit. Abdulhamid II, the last Sultan to hold real sway

over the Ottoman Empire, a great fan of detective stories, was an admirer. (In 1907 he received Sir Arthur Conan Doyle in Istanbul and decorated the author with a medal.)

It is no exaggeration to say that Sherlock Holmes's detective methods—leaving aside his almost preternatural talent for deductive reasoning—were groundbreaking. In recognition of his contribution to forensics, in 2002 the Royal Society of Chemistry went so far as to award the master detective a posthumous honorary fellowship, saying he was "way beyond his time in using chemistry and chemical sciences as a means of cracking crime. Many years ago, Holmes was using what would one day be forensic science in detection."

But what arrant nonsense! Posthumous? Everyone knows that Sherlock Holmes lives.

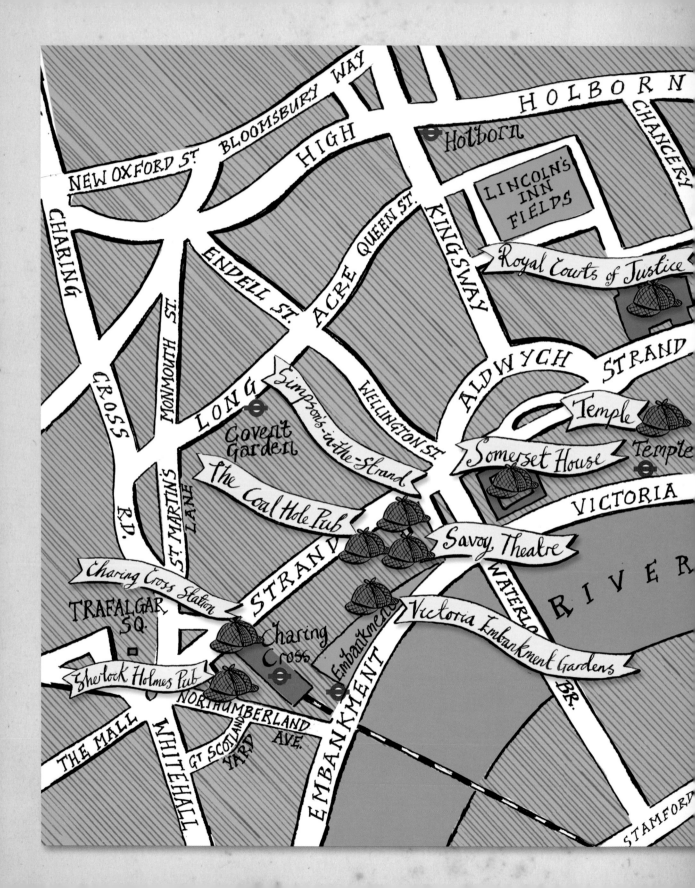

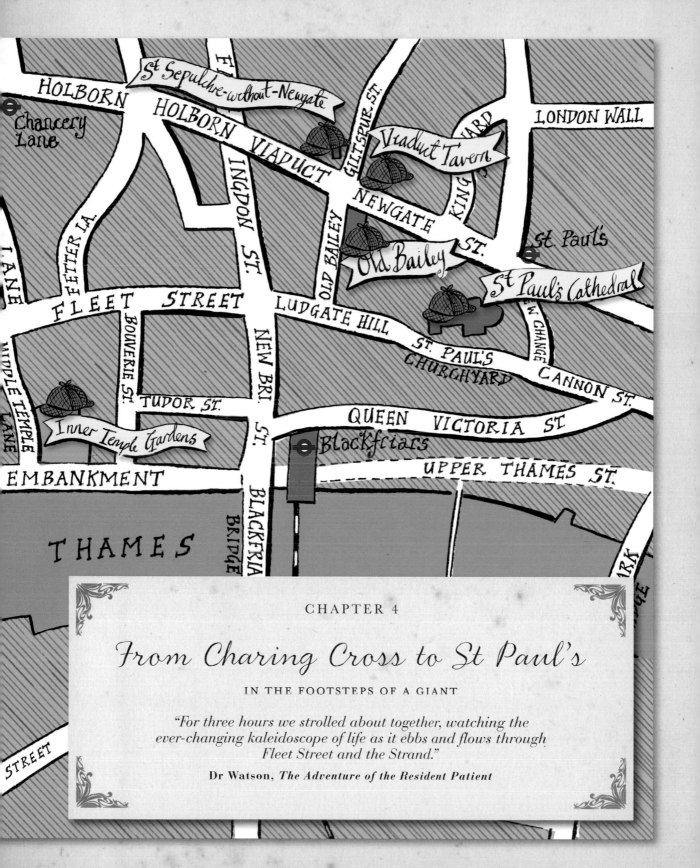

HOLBORN

Chancery Lane

St Sepulchre-without-Newgate

HOLBORN VIADUCT

GILTSPUR ST.

Viaduct Tavern

KING EDWARD ST.

LONDON WALL

FETTER LA.

INGDON ST.

OLD BAILEY

NEWGATE

ST. Paul's

Old Bailey

St Paul's Cathedral

FLEET STREET

LANE

LUDGATE HILL

ST. PAUL'S

BOUVERIE ST.

NEW BRI.

ST. PAUL'S CHURCHYARD

CHANGE

CANNON ST.

MIDDLE TEMPLE LANE

Inner Temple Gardens

TUDOR ST.

ST.

QUEEN VICTORIA ST.

Blackfriars

EMBANKMENT

BLACKFRIA BRIDGE

UPPER THAMES ST.

THAMES

RK

CHAPTER 4

From Charing Cross to St Paul's

IN THE FOOTSTEPS OF A GIANT

"For three hours we strolled about together, watching the ever-changing kaleidoscope of life as it ebbs and flows through Fleet Street and the Strand."

Dr Watson, *The Adventure of the Resident Patient*

From our very first acquaintance with Dr Watson, who was then residing in a private hotel there, the Strand was to make frequent appearances in the adventures of Sherlock Holmes. One of London's foremost thoroughfares, just three-quarters of a mile (1.2km) long, it borders the theater district, and with Fleet Street forms a conduit between the West End and the City.

Charing Cross Station, our starting point, is the official center of London. Built on the site of the old Hungerford Market, it co-opted Isambard Kingdom Brunel's suspension footbridge to make its river crossing, from 1859. The French Renaissance-style Charing Cross Hotel, above the station, was designed by EM Barry, son of Charles. The monument on the forecourt is an 1865 reimagining by Barry of one of the 12 "Eleanor

Crosses" erected by Edward I in memory of his queen, Eleanor of Castile, at the resting points of the funeral cortege from Lincoln to London in 1290. (The original, in Whitehall, was destroyed by Puritans in 1647.) The station appears in a number of Holmes stories. He was "white with chagrin" on learning, in *A Scandal in Bohemia,* that Irene Adler and her new husband had fled for the Continent, leaving on the 5.15am from Charing Cross. And in *The Man with the Twisted Lip* he declared himself "one of the most absolute fools in Europe. I deserve to be kicked from here to Charing Cross."

Before we follow in the footsteps of doctor and detective, we look in at the Victorian **Sherlock Holmes** pub at 10 Northumberland Street, which runs between the Strand and Northumberland Avenue. Whether or not this was the Northumberland Hotel, where Sir Henry

Baskerville stayed in *The Hound of the Baskervilles*, and where Sherlock inspected the visitors' book in pursuit of Francis Hay Moulton in *The Adventure of the Noble Bachelor*, it has to be seen. Formerly the Northumberland Arms, it is permanent home to an exhibition assembled for the Festival of Britain in 1951, acquired lock, stock, and barrel (in the shape of Dr Watson's old service revolver) by the brewery. There is the stuffed and mounted head of the hound that so terrified the Baskervilles,

OPPOSITE: On the forecourt of Charing Cross Station is a reimagined replica of the Eleanor Cross erected by Edward I in memory of his queen—but the story that Charing is a corruption of the French *chère reine* (dear queen) is apocryphal.

BELOW: The cozy sitting room, with a somewhat disturbing effigy of Sherlock Holmes, is displayed at the Sherlock Holmes pub, lovingly maintained since it was created as part of an exhibition for the Festival of Britain back in 1951.

cartoons, and TV and movie stills of actors who have played Holmes and Watson down the decades. Buy a souvenir deerstalker hat at the bar, but perhaps pass up Mrs Hudson's steak and ale pie or Moriarty's beef burger if you aspire to eat at Holmes's favorite restaurant.

Off Northumberland Avenue, on **Great Scotland Yard**, is the location of the rear entrance to the original headquarters of the Metropolitan Police at 4 Whitehall Place. It was this entrance that the public used—hence the force's nickname Scotland Yard. When, in 1890, the police HQ moved to new offices (page 42) the name went with it. Holmes, of course, had many dealings with the Yard's finest, and was moved to laughter when an apoplectic Dr Grimesby Roylott called him "Holmes the meddler… the Scotland Yard Jack-in-office" in *The Adventure of the Speckled Band*.

GAIETY, SONG, AND DANCE

In the 1890s the Strand was lined with music halls, theaters, and theater restaurants—the Tivoli, the Adelphi, the Gaiety… The "brightest beacon of all the pleasure lights of London," "that spark which lit the light of burlesque," the Gaiety at the Aldwych end of the Strand never failed to live up to its name. It was the creation of a Hoxton man, John Hollingshead, who managed it from 1868 to 1886, and made its name for musical comedy, burlesque, and operetta. In particular it was famous for the Gaiety Girls, its gorgeously attired dancers who were the envy of fashionable London. Hollingshead styled himself "licensed dealer in legs, short skirts, French adaptations, Shakespeare, taste and musical glasses."

At the Gaiety began one of the greatest theatrical collaborations of all time, when in 1871 Hollingshead brought together the librettist William Schwenck Gilbert and the composer Arthur Sullivan for a Christmas entertainment entitled *Thespis, or the Gods Grown Old*. Gilbert and Sullivan followed up with *Trial by Jury* and soon passed into legend. The producer Richard D'Oyly Carte encouraged the creative partnership that brought forth 14 comic operas including *HMS Pinafore*, *The Pirates of Penzance*, *The Mikado*, and *The Gondoliers*, which are still enrapturing audiences around the world.

In 1879 Carte founded the opera company that later became known as the D'Oyly Carte Opera Company, and in 1881 built the **Savoy Theatre** (Savoy Court, Strand) in 1881 to present what came to be called the "Savoy Operas." Things fell apart in 1890, with Gilbert suing Carte over his lax accounting and the money spent on carpeting for the theater. Sullivan supported Carte, and the rift never really healed. What never? Well, hardly ever. They collaborated on two last works, *Utopia Limited* and *The Grand Duke*, but failed to recapture their old brilliance.

Look sharp as you cross Savoy Court—the only road in London where traffic drives on the right.

ABOVE: "A mixture of pretty girls, English humor, singing, dancing and bathing machines and dresses of the English fashion" was how an American newspaper described the magic of the Gaiety. The Gaiety Girls' stage costumes were designed by top couturiers.

It is the private approach to D'Oyly Carte's Savoy Hotel, built with the takings from his Gilbert and Sullivan productions, and was a wonder of the age when it opened in 1889, complete with electric lights and lifts. By driving on the right, the chauffeur could hop down from his carriage and open the door for his lordship or her ladyship, without having to walk around the vehicle. Another little London mystery solved!

A quirky pub, **The Coal Hole** (91–2 Strand), is named after the 19th-century Coal Hole tavern that was very close by, in Fountain Court alleyway (now called Savoy Buildings). It had at one time been used as a coal store for the Savoy Hotel, but

ABOVE: Gilbert and Sullivan were at the height of their powers when *Princess Ida* (a satire on feminism, based on a poem by Alfred, Lord Tennyson) followed *Iolanthe* and preceded *The Mikado*. But a scorching summer undermined ticket sales.

in Holmes's day it was among a number of song-and-supper clubs, where customers were encouraged to sing comic favorites or croon sentimental ballads. It was home to the Wolf Club, founded by the actor Edmund Kean, for henpecked husbands denied by their wives the simple pleasure of singing in the bath.

"Amberley excelled at chess," says Holmes in *The Adventure of the Retired Colorman*, "one mark, Watson,

ABOVE: Check it out. A historic landmark restaurant, Simpson's-in-the-Strand was founded in 1828 as a chess club and coffee house. Liveried waiters trundling trolleys of roast meat over carpeted acres were instituted to avoid distracting the players. Holmes lunched here, in the gentlemen's dining room.

of a scheming mind." In 1828 The Grand Cigar Divan on the Strand opened its doors to Londoners with scheming minds, as a chess club and coffee house, soon acclaimed as "the home of chess." Its practice of wheeling joints of meat to diners' tables on silver-domed trolleys was contrived to avoid distracting the players. More recently, as **Simpson's-in-the-Strand**, it became a favored haunt of Holmes. Although no gourmet (when he was on a case he begrudged the energy required for digestion), he repaired there for "something nutritious" in *The Adventure of the Dying Detective.* In *The Adventure of the Illustrious Client* we

find him "at Simpson's… sitting at a small table in the front window and looking down at the rushing stream of life in the Strand." In fact, the ladies' dining room was upstairs, the gentlemen's below.

Simpson's was known to Charles Dickens, to George Bernard Shaw, and, of course, to Doyle himself. In 1899 it was already "old-fashioned" according to one contemporary reviewer, who reported that "with its imitation marble columns, its colored tile floor, its trees in tubs… Simpson's does not look like a place that changes." Nor has it, so very much. Waiters are still "Britannic" and dignified. The napery and drapery, deep upholstery, chandeliers and coffered ceilings, speak of luxury. Our Victorian diner enjoyed stewed eels and Liebfraumilch, but most people go for "the best roast beef and lamb in the country"—and dress smartly. More modern fare—honey panko prawns, BBQ pork spare ribs, Simpson's burger—is available in the Knight's Bar. (At the time of going to press, Simpson's was up for sale—readers must do their own detective work to see if it remains the same.)

Just beyond Waterloo Bridge is a Neoclassical masterpiece, **Somerset House**. Designed by William Chambers in the reign of George III as "a great public building" and "object of national splendor," it has housed the Royal Academy of Arts, the Society of Antiquaries, the Navy Board, and (in the days when it had direct access to the Thames) the King's Bargemaster. By the time Holmes and Watson ambled by, it was the headquarters of the Inland Revenue. They would wonder to see it today, in winter, when the courtyard is transformed into a torch-lit ice rink. A popular filming location, it can be seen in the 1970 movie *The Private Life of Sherlock Holmes*, and in the 2009 *Sherlock Holmes*, starring Robert Downey Jr, when the bowels of the building stood in for Pentonville Prison.

The last stop before Fleet Street is the Gothic Revival stone edifice designed by George Edmund Street in the 1870s, the **Royal Courts of Justice**. This is where, fittingly, in 2012, the judgment was handed down that Undershaw—the home in Hindhead, Surrey, that Sir Arthur Conan Doyle helped to design and where he breathed life back into the "dead" Sherlock—could not be redeveloped as eight separate dwellings.

WHAT LIES BENEATH

The Strand, as the name suggests, was once a waterside promenade. Below it, running parallel, is a pleasant walk with Holmes associations. The Victoria Embankment was created in the 1860s by Joseph Bazalgette, chief engineer at the Metropolitan Board of Works. The Italianate York Watergate, dating from 1626, which is at the foot of Buckingham Street in Embankment Gardens, was one of a number of watergates left high and dry when Bazalgette narrowed and rerouted the Thames as part of what was then the most ambitious civil engineering project in the world.

Beneath the Embankment are sections of Bazalgette's sewage system—82 miles (132km) of brick-lined conduits designed to carry the waste that was formerly discharged into the stinking, insalubrious Thames, away to outlying pumping stations and treatment plants. (One of these, Crossness Pumping Station, provided a backdrop for the filming of the 2009 *Sherlock Holmes* movie, when Blackwood descended to the sewers.)

BELOW: Children at play in the Embankment Gardens. Planted in soil reclaimed from the river with the building of Joseph Bazalgette's Embankment, the gardens are overlooked by EM Barry's French-Renaissance-style Charing Cross Hotel, as London sewage is spirited away beneath, to outlying treatment plants.

The "sewer chase" was shot at the underground reservoir at Finsbury Park, north London.)

The granite Egyptian obelisk on the Embankment, although flanked by 19th-century faux-Egyptian bronze sphinxes, is the real thing—hewn, carved, and engraved for the pharaoh Thutmose III in 1460 BC. Known as Cleopatra's Needle, it is one of a pair that stood before the Temple of the Sun at Heleopolis. (Its sister is in Central Park, New York.) It had been lying, toppled, for centuries in Alexandria when it was presented to the British Nation in 1819 by the Viceroy of Egypt. It arrived in London in 1878, the huge shipping cost having eventually been raised by public subscription, and was erected in commemoration of British victory over the six Napoleons in 1815.

The pedestal for the obelisk, the two bronze sphinxes, the cast-iron benches with winged-sphinx armrests, and the "dolphin" lamps along the Victoria Embankment were all designed by the architect George Vulliamy in anticipation of the obelisk's arrival. In the end, this was only after a storm-tossed voyage that nearly saw it lost in the Bay of Biscay. Under the obelisk is buried a time capsule, containing, it is said, children's toys, coins, a portrait of Queen Victoria, golden pince-nez, copies of ten daily newspapers, the Bible, tobacco pipes, a man's suit, a rupee, and a beryl coronet.

It was from the Embankment that John Openshaw was thrown in the river in *The Five Orange Pips* and—though a police constable on Waterloo Bridge heard the splash—could not be rescued.

In the summer in Embankment Gardens, lunchtime crowds lounge in deckchairs and enjoy bandstand concerts—Swing Dance in the Park, Tour de Brass, the Speckled Band, the London Gay Symphonic Winds—blissfully unmindful of the tons of ordure flowing beneath. As a metaphor for London in the age of Sherlock Holmes, this could not be bettered.

On Carting Lane, which leads alongside the Savoy up to the Strand, stands London's only remaining Webb Patent Sewer Gas Lamp. These days it is fueled by mains gas, although sewer gases drawn up through a flue are also burned off. It is characteristic of a certain brand of London humor that this cut-through has been nicknamed "Farting Lane."

FLEET AFOOT

From the Royal Courts of Justice we continue down Fleet Street, still shorthand for the national press, despite the exodus of newspaper publishers since the late 1980s. The street itself is named for the subterranean Fleet, the largest of London's "lost rivers." The sublime prospect of Sir Christopher Wren's masterwork, St Paul's Cathedral, is always in view.

On the south side of Fleet Street is a pub with the narrowest frontage of any in London, Ye Olde Cock Tavern, which moved to the site from across the road in 1887. In its previous incarnation it was known to the diarist Samuel Pepys, and to lexicographer Samuel Johnson, whose Georgian house may be seen, with a statue of his cat, Hodge, by following Johnson's Court off to the left, to Gough Square.

On the north side of Fleet Street, on Wine Office Court, is Ye Olde Cheshire Cheese, another of the "host of hostelries" that used to cater to the notoriously thirsty journalists. If Holmes and Watson had stopped off, they might have dined on stewed cheese, or rump-steak pudding washed down with a bowl of punch. Doyle certainly knew this higgledy-piggledy old place, with its staircases, corridors, and jumble of rooms, rebuilt in 1666 after the Great Fire.

Maybe among the numbers of back alleys Johnson's or Wine Office Courts stood in for "Pope's Court," which Jabez Wilson found "choked with red-headed folk" and looking "like a coster's orange barrow," as hopefuls queued at the bogus offices of the Red-Headed League in the story of the same name.

Between Fleet St and the Embankment lies the **Temple**, the name recalling the secretive 12th-

ABOVE: Sir Christopher Wren's masterpiece, St Paul's Cathedral, is constantly in view from Fleet Street. Less seen, and not visible here, is "Wren's madrigal," St Bride's, the journalists' church, tucked away just behind Fleet Street, which was the home of the first printing press. Its spire is said to have been the inspiration for the tiered wedding cake.

century Knights Templar, who built the medieval Temple Church, one of the oldest in London, modeled on the circular Church of the Holy Sepulchre in Jerusalem. The Temple is a sequestered base for the legal profession, with two of the four Inns of Court, Inner Temple and Middle Temple, located here. The essayist Charles Lamb (1775–1834) spent his first seven years in the Inner Temple and his later evocation of "the most elegant spot in the metropolis" with its "unexpected

avenues," "magnificent ample squares," and "classic green recesses" rings no less true today. Dark, handsome Godfrey Norton, fiancé and accomplice of Irene Adler, had chambers at the **Inner Temple** in *A Scandal in Bohemia*.

Middle Temple Lane is another "star" of the 2009 *Sherlock Holmes* movie. Seen from the Embankment, it is framed by an exuberant archway designed by EM Barry. Replete with cherubs, and with Holmes's friends "Learning" and "Justice"

personified by statues in niches, the arch was dismissed as a "vulgar monstrosity" in 1878. For wigs and gowns barristers can pop over to Chancery Lane to shop at Ede & Ravenscroft, purveyors of legal regalia and paraphernalia since 1689.

From Ludgate Circus we continue up Ludgate Hill to **St Paul's Cathedral**, which commands the highest vantage in the City. The exterior shots in the 2009 movie *Sherlock Holmes* give a sense of the immensity of Wren's masterpiece. The spiral staircase leading to the crypt in the film was in reality the stairs of the southwest tower, where

hangs "Great Paul," at 16.5 tons the largest bell ever cast in the British Isles. It has been silent these past few years because of a broken chiming mechanism. The movie's crypt scene, in which Lord Blackwood prepares a human sacrifice, was actually shot in the nave of the church of St Bartholomew the Great, up the road in Smithfield.

If you descend to St Paul's crypt you will find not bats and cobwebs but a modern restaurant, café, and shop. Among impressive tombs is that of the cathedral's architect, Sir Christopher Wren. A plaque on the wall above bears an epitaph in

OPPOSITE: A map of the Temple, with Fleet Street to the north, shows the river bordered by beautifully ordered gardens. Dated 1871, the artwork was already history. The Embankment had been completed the year before, cutting the Inns of court off from the Thames.

BELOW RIGHT: Fair lady. Frederick Pomeroy's statue of Justice stands above the dome of the Old Bailey. In her left hand are the scales to weigh evidence, and in her right the double-edged sword of Reason and Justice.

Latin, which translates as "Reader, if you would seek his monument, look around you."

From Ludgate Hill, a left turn onto Old Bailey, named for the old city wall or "bailey," takes you to the Central Criminal Court, commonly known as **the Old Bailey**. Its dome is a small echo of St Paul's, topped with its own gilded, cruciform figure, the Lady of Justice, with a sword in one hand, scales in the other. The present, Baroque-style building dates from 1902–7 and stands partly on the site of the notorious Newgate Prison, but there has been a court of some description here since the 16th century.

The Old Bailey was where the most heinous—or misjudged—criminals stood trial and faced execution. In the "Reichenbach Fall" episode of BBC's *Sherlock* the exterior is shown (the interiors were shot at Swansea Guildhall in Wales). If you care to see British justice in action, the public galleries are open on weekdays (no under-14s). Trials were ever a spectator sport—in the days when they were conducted in the open air at the Bailey, with the judge seated in a portico, they could be compared to a giant Punch and Judy show, with His Honor cast as that old wife-beater Mr Punch.

The Viaduct Tavern on the corner of Newgate Street is wonderfully ornate. The claim in various guidebooks that primitive cages in the cellar are former Newgate cells is almost certainly misleading.

Just to the left, on Holborn Viaduct, is the church **of St Sepulchre-without-Newgate** ("the bells of Old Bailey" in the nursery rhyme "Oranges and Lemons"). The great bell tolled as condemned men and women were led to the gallows after their last sleepless night on earth. Preserved in a glass case is the "Execution Bell," which in the 18th century was rung by a bellman at midnight on the eve of an execution, outside the condemned cell, as he recited to the tormented souls in the cell a reminder (lest it slipped their minds), this woeful piece of doggerel:

All you that in the Condemn'd hold do lie,
Prepare you, for to-morrow you shall die…

If you go back down Old Bailey and turn left on Ludgate Hill, the next left is Ave Maria Lane. Monks reciting the Lord's Prayer as they processed from Paternoster ("Our Father") Row to St Paul's, upon the feast of Corpus Christi, would say their "amen" here. It leads to the secluded enclave of Amen Court. The dark and looming wall you see at the rear, partly hidden by bushes, is a surviving wall of the "two great, windowless" blocks of Newgate Prison. In Holmes's day, Newgate was no longer used for long-term prisoners, only for those awaiting trial or whose fate was the hangman's noose.

IN DURANCE VILE

ondon's Bastille, Newgate struck sick terror in the hearts of those who so much as walked past it. The cockney phrase "as black as Newgate's knocker" expresses the dread that it inspired. When the doors of Newgate opened to admit a felon, Hell yawned. Some who passed through them would never emerge. The "graveyard" for executed prisoners was the passage between the prison and the Old Bailey; the coffins, in which lime was enclosed with the bodies, were interred under the flagstones, the deceased's initials scratched upon the wall by way of record.

Charles Dickens was granted a guided tour and wrote a powerful evocation of what lay within this "gloomy depository of guilt and misery," of "tortuous and intricate windings, guarded in their turn by huge gates and gratings, whose appearance is sufficient to dispel at once the slightest hope of escape." The sight of the condemned pew in the meanly appointed chapel would afterward come between him and sleep. He saw 25 or 30 prisoners under sentence of death, "men of all ages and appearances from a hardened old offender with swarthy face and grizzly beard" to "a handsome boy, not fourteen years old, and of singularly youthful appearance, even for that age, who had been condemned for burglary."

There is no record of what retribution awaited all the criminals—blackmailers, thieves, murderers— whom Sherlock Holmes outwitted. He seems not to have dwelt upon it, being content that the law would take its course. In a rare instance of speculation, in *The Adventure of the Retired Colorman*, he suggested that, with his very unusual mentality, Josiah Amberley's destination was "more likely to be Broadmoor than the scaffold"—a reference to Broadmoor Criminal Lunatic Asylum in Berkshire, which had opened in 1864.

Draconian punishments, appalling prison conditions, and execution seem to have been no deterrent to those wrongdoers who had the hubris to imagine that they could outwit not just the police but the world's first consulting detective. (Amberley, we recall, actually engaged Holmes to find the wife he had murdered—how mad was *that*!)

OPPOSITE: The graveyard shift. From 1868 hangings were carried out (sometimes three at a time) within Newgate, and the bodies buried under the flagstones of "Dead Men's Walk," a corridor connecting prison and adjoining courts. Stone walls do very much a prison make.

RIGHT: Welcome to purgatory. The chief warder and his assistant at the prison's inner door. When the tenor bell of St Sepulchre-without-Newgate tolled, all within heard it and knew that it signaled an execution. Seek not to ask for whom the bell tolls…

Arthur Conan Doyle, if he was ever stuck for an idea, had only to read the newspapers for lurid tales of true-life criminals, some more bizarre than any fiction. Who could have invented the character Charles Peace, mentioned by Holmes in *The Adventure of the Illustrious Client* ("My old friend Charlie Peace was a violin virtuoso")? The son of a one-legged lion tamer, Peace was a cat burglar, escapologist, murderer, and master of disguise. Such

was his ability to alter his physiognomy that Scotland Yard variously stated his age at from 40 to 70. He stood just 5 feet 4 inches (1.6m) tall and walked with a pronounced limp yet was a limber acrobat. After a finger was shot off, he wore a fake arm. (Really, you couldn't make it up!) By day he earned a living reciting Shakespearean soliloquies and playing a one-stringed violin in pubs and at fairs; by night he burgled houses, carrying the tools of his trade in his violin case, along with spiked meat to drug guard dogs. He was several times imprisoned in a 25-year career too eventful to be told here, was hanged at Armley Prison in West Yorkshire on February 25, 1879, aged 47, and was immortalized in the Chamber of Horrors.

Also immortalized at Madame Tussauds, although for different reasons, and in more honorable estate, is Britain's most celebrated prison detainee of that day, and its most articulate. Oscar Wilde was sentenced on May 25, 1895, to two years' hard labor for indecency, three months after the curtain went up on his most famous play, *The Importance of Being Earnest.*

BELOW: An effigy of the notorious hanged murderer, escapologist, acrobat, and "virtuoso violinist" Charles Peace is carried from Madame Tussauds in 1930 to preside as "honorary president" over an evening meeting of the Crime Club.

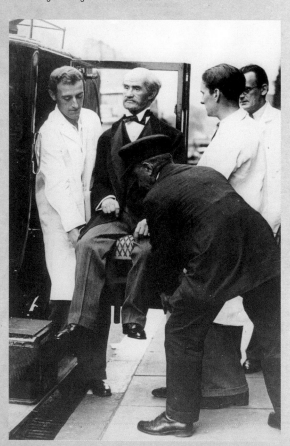

ABOVE: Oscar Wilde in exile on the Continent, where he suffered depression and lost his joy in writing. "This poverty really breaks one's heart," he wrote to his publisher. He was to die of cerebral meningitis in a dingy backstreet hotel in Paris, with one last waspish quip: "Either that wallpaper goes or I do."

ABOVE: Oscar Wilde was always a gift to cartoonists, who lampooned his foppish appearance and flamboyant antics. This particularly cruel satire shows him before his fall from grace—and afterward, a pathetic and decrepit figure bound for exile with scant possessions.

Inmates were fed near-starvation rations of weak gruel, badly baked bread, suet, and water, as Wilde wrote to the *Daily Chronicle* after his release:

"Nothing can be worse than the sanitary arrangements of English prisons. Every prisoner suffers day and night from hunger. A certain amount of food is carefully weighed out ounce by ounce for each prisoner. It is just enough to sustain, not life exactly, but existence. But one is always racked by the pain and sickness of hunger.

The present prison system seems almost to have for its aim the wrecking and the destruction of the mental faculties. The production of insanity is, if not its object, certainly its result... Deprived of books, of all human intercourse, isolated from every humane and humanizing influence, condemned to eternal silence, robbed of all intercourse with the external world, treated like an unintelligent animal, brutalized below the level of any of the brute-creation, the wretched man who is confined in an English prison can hardly escape becoming insane."

Wilde was to spend the last three years of his life in Paris, dying bankrupt, aged 46. He is buried at Père Lachaise cemetery. One could weep to think of how far he had fallen from the glitzy, glamorous champagne days at the Café Royal, the days of promise when he and Doyle were lunched and feted at the Langham— all for the love that dare not speak its name.

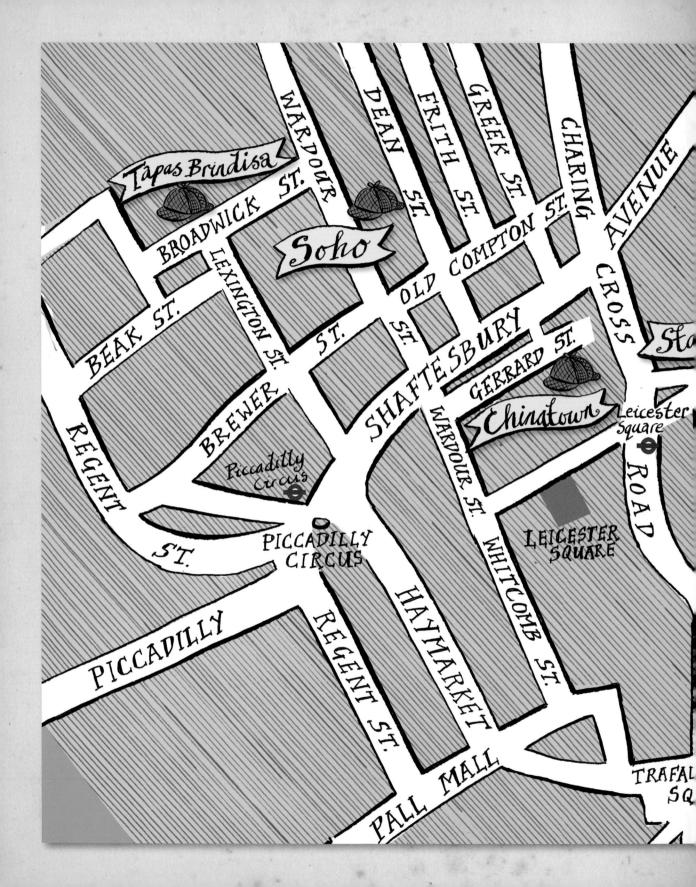

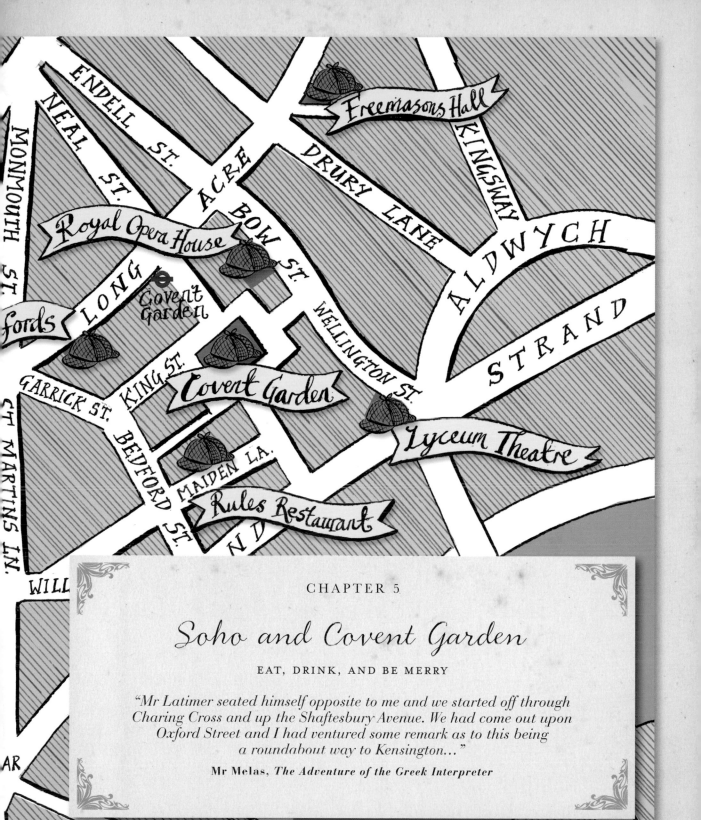

CHAPTER 5

Soho and Covent Garden

EAT, DRINK, AND BE MERRY

"Mr Latimer seated himself opposite to me and we started off through Charing Cross and up the Shaftesbury Avenue. We had come out upon Oxford Street and I had ventured some remark as to this being a roundabout way to Kensington…"

Mr Melas, *The Adventure of the Greek Interpreter*

A roundabout way indeed! Shaftesbury Avenue does not lead from Charing Cross—but, then, Mr Melas was being kidnapped, taken on a nightmare journey, and menaced by Latimer who took out a bludgeon and drew up the carriage windows, which were covered with paper. We should not wonder that he was confused.

Shaftesbury Avenue runs from Piccadilly Circus to New Oxford Street, slicing clean through Soho. Named for the social reformer Anthony Ashley Cooper, 7th Earl of Shaftesbury, and completed in 1886, it was the work of the architect George Vulliamy and the engineer Joseph Bazalgette (see page 69), part of a slum-clearance operation to displace impoverished families from the city center. It is lined with theaters. The oldest of them, the Lyric, opened in 1888 with a comic opera entitled *Dorothy*. In the second episode of the first series of the BBC's *Sherlock*, "The Blind Banker", Holmes and Watson bump into one another by a bus stop close to Piccadilly Circus before heading up to Chinatown.

Soho is no great distance from highbrow Bloomsbury or high-class St James's; it is merely a world away. Comprising a warren of streets, bounded by mighty Regent Street and Oxford Street to the west and north, and Charing Cross Road to the east, it has always been a bit raffish, louche, permissive, bohemian. A German nobleman, Count E Armfelt, wrote in 1903:

"No part of the world presents in such a small area so many singular and interesting pictures of cosmopolitan life as Soho, which is the cherished home of foreign artists, dancers, musicians, singers, and other talented performers, and the sanctuary of political refugees, conspirators, deserters and defectors of all nations."

The name recalls the days of the 17th century when this was open countryside and echoed to the cries of huntsmen—"So-*ho*!" Today's visitors come hunting not for foxes but for fresh pasta, salami, olive oil, and *biscotti* at I Camisa & Son (61 Old

ABOVE: "What a lovely thing a rose is!" says Holmes in *The Adventure of the Naval Treaty*. He might have bought a moss rose from any number of "flower girls" eking out a living on the London streets. Not all were young. Here an older florist sets out her stall under the statue of Eros on Piccadilly Circus.

Compton Street) and Lina Stores (18 Brewer Street); for fruit and veg and street food at Berwick Street Market; for coffee at Algerian Coffee Stores (52 Old Compton Street), established in 1887; for a Meow eye mask, whips, paddles, and saucy lingerie at Agent Provocateur (6 Broadwick Street). "Human nature is a strange mixture, Watson."

Soho had long had a French community, with a settlement of Huguenots in what was then Leicester Fields in around 1700, but the 1890s saw an influx of Germans, Italians, Swiss, Jewish refugees from Eastern Europe, even Scandinavians, bringing with them their culture and customs. "Everywhere in Soho there are

ABOVE: Pasta master. Luigi Azario's Florence on Rupert Street was the largest Italian restaurant in Soho. Holmes, for preference, dined at the "garish" Goldini's, west London, as he pondered the missing pages of the Bruce-Partington Plans, summoning Watson to join him—bringing jemmy, dark lantern, chisel, and revolver.

queer announcements of foreign wares and eatables," Count Armfelt continued. Restaurants opened to feed homesick migrants (with rooms above often leased to prostitutes,) offering native Londoners a taste of exotic foods at very reasonable prices—so the after-theater supper craze was born.

Among the "political refugees, conspirators, deserters and defectors" of the late 1800s was Emidio Recchioni, an anarchist from Ravenna who fled to London in 1898, set up a grocery store, King Bomba, on Old Compton Street, and later funded two attempts on the life of Mussolini.

Naturally communists gravitated to Soho. A prime mover within the red circle, Karl Marx, who lived at 28 Dean Street, worked with Frederick Engels on *The Communist Manifesto* in an upstairs room at the Red Lion on the corner of Great Windmill Street. It is a sign of the times that it is now a trendy cocktail bar, its history effaced.

Thank goodness Soho's cosmopolitan air survives, along with a great choice of restaurants.

Where else to start but **Tapas Brindisa** at 46 Broadwick Street (slightly rebranded since it doubled for Angelo's in *Sherlock*)?

On the other side of—and running parallel to—Shaftesbury Avenue are Gerrard Street and Lisle Street, at the heart of **Chinatown.** In the 1890s London's small Cantonese community of mainly single males congregated in Limehouse in the East End, where Chinese sailors bringing cargoes of tea sometimes settled. In *The Adventure of the Dying Detective*, Holmes devised a ruse to entrap Culverton Smith with the story that he has contracted a deadly Asian disease while working among Chinese seamen in the docks.

From the 1970s, with the growing popularity of Chinese food among Londoners, and an influx of immigrants from Hong Kong, restaurateurs gravitated westward. You'll find not just Chinese restaurants but bakers, supermarkets, and souvenir shops. There are bilingual street signs, a pagoda, traditional Chinese arches, and everywhere Chinese lanterns. The enclave is familiar from the BBC's *Sherlock*: in "The Blind Banker" episode, Holmes and Watson investigate the antics of a Chinese smuggling ring. (However, the Lucky Cat Emporium was shot in Newport, Wales.)

If you head north on Shaftesbury Avenue, a left turn onto Charing Cross Road would lead to Tottenham Court Road, where Henry Baker was set upon by roughs in *The Adventure of the Blue Carbuncle* and where Holmes bought from a pawnbroker, for 55 shillings, a Stradivarius worth "at least 500 guineas", as he related to Watson in *The Adventure of the Cardboard Box.* It is not suggested that we go there in search of similar bargains.

Just as Shaftesbury Avenue is about theater, Charing Cross Road is about bookshops—new, secondhand, or antiquarian, rare or mass-market. Foyles, at No. 107, was once the largest bookshop in the world, with 30 miles (50km) of shelves. In recent years high rents have been killing off the booksellers—including, ironically the crime fiction specialist Murder One, and, very sadly, Marks & Co, the legendary 84 Charing Cross Road of book and movie fame (at present, a Belgian chain restaurant).

GARDEN OF DELIGHTS

Heading south on Charing Cross Road, a left onto Great Newport Street brings us to Long Acre and a venerable business that was well known to Holmes. In *The Hound of the Baskervilles* he confessed he had been doing a little armchair traveling, visiting Devon in his mind over two large pots of coffee and "an incredible amount of tobacco," having "sent down to Stamford's [sic] for the Ordnance map of this portion of the moor." **Stanfords** began as London's only map seller, on Charing Cross Road, and has grown into *the* London travel shop, a wonderful resource for maps, guides, atlases, travel literature, destination-led fiction, world globes, gifts, and more.

In 1862 the company founder, Edward Stanford, published what the Royal Geographical Society hailed as "the most perfect map of London that has ever been issued"—a work of beauty, compiled with the help of a team of surveyors, and still on sale. The shop has occupied its premises here on the site of its former printing works, at 12–14 Long Acre, since 1901. It claims among its former clients Florence Nightingale (bound for Scutari?), David Livingstone (off to Africa, we presume)—and you know who.

Continuing up Long Acre, **Endell Street**, on the left, leads up to High Holborn. In *The Adventure of the Blue Carbuncle* Holmes and Watson passed down it from Holborn, "and so through a zigzag of slums to the Covent Garden Market." Covent Garden was the fruit and vegetable wholesale market. It moved across the river to Nine Elms in 1974, and Covent Garden became a smart tourist destination—no slums now, no cauliflower stalks or cabbage leaves!

Long Acre leads into Great Queen Street, with the **Freemasons' Hall** at No. 60. Headquarters

Covent Garden Market, London

of the United Grand Wisteria Lodge, it appeared in Guy Ritchie's 2009 *Sherlock Holmes*, but it is not as the flame-haired Jabez Wilson, or Enoch Drebber or Inspector Barker—Freemasons all—would have known it. It dates from 1933 and is one of the finest Art Deco buildings in Britain. No need to roll up a trouser leg or give a secret handshake   it is open to non-masons ("the profane") and free tours are available.

Returning to the junction, take a left and head south, as Holmes and Watson did, on Bow Street. **The Royal Opera House** on the right, with its grandiose Corinthian portico, is where our two friends caught the second act on Wagner night upon the satisfactory conclusion of *The Adventure of the Red Circle*. Designed by EM Barry, the building dates from 1858 and was the third theater on the site. It is home to both the Royal

ABOVE LEFT: Charles Fowler's classical Covent Garden market building surrounded by wholesalers' wagons. The former convent kitchen garden, "where a salad was cut for a lady abbess," wrote Walter Savage Landor, "becomes a market, noisy and full of life, distributing thousands of fruits and vegetables to a vicious metropolis."

ABOVE RIGHT: The imposing portico of EM Barry's Royal Opera House, with his glass-and-iron Floral Hall beyond. Replacing a building that burned down in 1856, it opened in 1858 with a performance of Meyerbeer's *Les Huguenots*, the opera Holmes enjoyed in *The Hound of the Baskervilles*

Opera and the Royal Ballet. The delicate bronze statue opposite, of a dancer tying her ballet shoe, is by Enzo Plazzotta.

Abutting the Royal Opera House is Barry's barrel-roofed glass-and-iron Floral Hall—or rather a rebuilding of it. It must have been thrilling to see it when it was as an exotic flower market—and terrible to see it burning in 1956, with the sound of glass panes exploding.

BOW STREET 1888

Bow Street was the birthplace of systematic criminal detection in the England of the mid-1700s, when the dramatist and novelist Henry Fielding (author of *Tom Jones*) was appointed as a magistrate, moving into the courthouse and residence at No. 4. With his blind half-brother and fellow magistrate, John, he instituted a new tradition of·justice and crime-fighting in London, recruiting a posse of "thief-takers" known as "Mr Fielding's people" (later the Bow Street Runners) and nicknamed the "Robin Redbreasts" for their red waistcoats. He launched a newspaper, *The Covent Garden Journal*, and through it exhorted victims of robbers and burglars to furnish him with the best descriptions they could, with details

of time, place, and circumstance. In the 1790s seven police offices, one of which was on Bow Street, were set up around London; each was staffed with magistrates and constables. A centralized force, the Metropolitan Police, was established in 1829—the direct descendants of the Bow Street Runners, who were disbanded ten years later.

It was to Bow Street that Holmes and Watson hastened by pony and trap, heading north over Waterloo Bridge and up Wellington Street, unaccountably "wheeling sharply to the right," in *The Man with the Twisted Lip*. Two constables at the door of the police court saluted Holmes, and he was taken to the cells to question Hugh Boone,

OPPOSITE: The "bobbies" of Bow Street in 1888. They were employed not just to apprehend criminals but also to control civil unrest, as in the Trafalgar Square riots of 1886 and 1887 known as "Black Monday" and "Bloody Sunday."

RIGHT: Crowds queue outside the Lyceum Theatre, where the schoolboy Arthur Conan Doyle saw Henry Irving play Hamlet. Bram Stoker was for 20 years business manager and was said to have taken Irving as his model for Count Dracula. Mary Morstan was to wait beside the third pillar in *The Sign of Four*.

aka Mr Neville St Clair, of Lee, in the county of Kent—unmasked by the vigorous application of a wet sponge to his filthy face.

Completed in 1881, the **Bow Street Magistrates' Court** building was sold off in 2004. At the time of writing it is to be converted to a boutique hotel, with a crime museum in the original police cells where St Clair was forced to come clean.

Down on Wellington Street, just off the Strand, is the **Lyceum Theatre**. In *The Sign of Four* Mary Morstan was instructed by letter to be at the third pillar from the left at 7pm. "If you are distrustful, bring two friends." It was at the Lyceum that, as a schoolboy, Arthur Conan Doyle saw Henry Irving play Hamlet. In previous incarnations the theater housed a circus, a chapel, and Madame Tussaud's first London exhibition of waxworks and French Revolution horrorbilia. It was also the HQ of the Sublime Society of Beef Steaks, a kind of meaty freemasonry, maximum 26 members, motto "Beef and Liberty!" In 1815 the Lyceum became the first British theater to have its stage lit by gas instead of oil lamps; it went up in smoke, and was rebuilt in 1834 to a design by Samuel Beazley. It was rebuilt again in 1904 but retained the Victorian facade with its grand portico. After World War II it became a ballroom and then a pop concert venue, but in 1996 was finally reconverted into a theater.

Walk west along the Strand, turn right on Southampton Street, then left onto Maiden Lane. At No. 35 is London's oldest restaurant, **Rules**, established by Thomas Rule in 1798. Sir John Betjeman, a poet and ardent conservationist, described it as "unique and irreplaceable... part of literary and theatrical London." The actor Henry Irving ate here. So did Charles Dickens, William Thackeray, and HG Wells. The food is traditional British—oysters, game, roasts, pies, puddings—and the interior old-fashioned, with plush red banquettes, red carpet, lamps, paintings...

Southampton Street leads to the Piazza, laid out by Inigo Jones in 1631 for the 4th Earl of Bedford, with Neoclassical market buildings designed two centuries later by Charles Fowler for the 6th Duke. Covent Garden was where Henry Baker bought his Christmas goose in *The Adventure of the Blue Carbuncle*. Today we find fashion shops, a perfumer, a chocolatier—but no geese.

OUT ON THE TOWN

"And now, my dear Watson... I think, we may turn our thoughts into more pleasant channels. I have a box for 'Les Huguenots.' Have you heard the De Reszkes? Might I trouble you then to be ready in half an hour, and we can stop at Marcini's for a little dinner on the way?"

Sherlock Holmes, *The Hound of the Baskervilles*

It would be too much to say that Sherlock sometimes let his hair down, but his knowledge of music was extensive, his love of it profound. For men and women of highbrow tastes, London was rich in cultural diversions. The opera was perhaps Holmes's foremost pleasure. We see that he admired the Polish tenor Jean de Reszke, whom he would see in Meyerbeer's *Les Huguenots*—although no one in the world of opera commanded the grudging admiration he felt for that devious diva Irene Adler after that notorious scandal in Bohemia.

The violin, his own instrument, on which he would scrape away or play with eccentric brilliance, naturally appealed. (He was, too, a composer of no ordinary merit.) In *A Study in Scarlet* he went to "Hallé's concert to hear Norman-Neruda" at St James's Hall in Piccadilly (since demolished). "The female Paganini," Wilhelmine Norman-Neruda (aka Wilma Neruda, who married the conductor Charles Hallé a few months after the publication of *A Study in Scarlet*), always played a Stradivarius, like Holmes. "Her attack and her bowing are splendid. What's that little thing of Chopin's she plays so magnificently? Tra-la-la-lira-lira-lay," he asked Watson as he leaned back in the cab and "caroled away like a lark."

He was back at St James's Hall in *The Red-Headed League* to hear the violinist Pablo de Sarasate: "I observe that there is a good deal of German music on the program, which is rather more to my taste than Italian or French. It is introspective, and I want to introspect." So he sat, all afternoon, "wrapped in the most perfect happiness, gently waving his long, thin fingers in time with the music," his gently smiling

face and languid, dreamy eyes suggesting to Watson that an evil time was ahead for his quarry.

PLAY TIME

The London theater scene was vibrant, with some 30 playhouses in the West End alone offering everything from light-hearted comedy and farce such as the hugely successful *Charley's Aunt*, to

RIGHT: Wilma (Wilhelmine) Norman-Neruda, later Lady Charles Hallé, defied a convention that the violin was no instrument for a woman. A great star in her time, she is today chiefly known from the mention of her in *A Study in Scarlet*.

ABOVE: Human billboards. Men hung with placards walk the Strand to advertise theater in the surrounding streets. The novelist Charles Dickens was the first to characterize them as sandwich men—"a piece of human flesh between two slices of paste board."

such challenging works as Ibsen's *A Doll's House.* With no cinema or even radio, stage dramas were great crowd-pleasers.

A lot of the excitement of theater lay with scenography, hydraulics, scene painting, set design, and special effects such as smoke and flares—while the new genre of "cup-and-saucer drama" went for realism. (The play *Ours* actually called for the onstage baking of a roly-poly pudding.)

In 1893, "A New and Original English Comic Opera in Two Acts," *Jane Annie or The Good Conduct Prize*, was produced at the Savoy Theatre,

with 50 performances staged there between May and July. The music was composed by Ernest Ford, the libretto by JM Barrie (later famed as the creator of Peter Pan) and his friend Arthur Conan Doyle. The critics were scathing: "Less a comic opera than a tragedy"; "Messrs Barrie and Conan Doyle have thoroughly exemplified how not to do it"; "Of plot it has none, and of humor very little"; "How could two able men make so great a mistake?"; "It would take the perspicacity of Sherlock Holmes himself to get at the meaning of it." George Bernard Shaw did not mince his words:

"the most unblushing outburst of tomfoolery that two responsible citizens could conceivably indulge in publicly."

It is as well that Holmes would not have attended such a low-brow entertainment as a comic opera, so was spared being audience to the Savoy Theatre's first unmitigated flop.

Drama could present a very public challenge to late Victorian mores and morals, and scripts were subject to censorship, for 20 years, under the arbitrary eye of Edward F Smyth Pigott, Chief Examiner of Plays for the Lord Chamberlain.

One drama that got under the censorship wire, *The Notorious Mrs Ebbsmith*, by Sir Arthur Wing Pinero, starred the beautiful, witty, and capricious Mrs Patrick Campbell. It premiered at the Garrick on March 13, 1895, and explored themes of social radicalism and free love, through the central character, a 33-year-old widow, Agnes Ebbsmith.

On May 28 the *Evening Post*, under the headline "A remarkable coincidence," reported that the body of a divorcée named Alice Ebb-Smith had been found in the river. In her pocket were two tickets for Pinero's play. Verdict: "Found drowned in the Thames." A case for Sherlock Holmes if ever there was one!

Spoofs and parodies were all the rage—whether sending up the cockney or the monocled toff. In 1893 at the Royal Court Theatre, Charles Brookfield became the first actor to parody Sherlock Holmes on stage, in *Under the Clock*, written by Brookfield and Seymour Hicks, with Hicks as Dr Watson, singing a duet, "You Wonderful Man!". Arthur Conan Doyle was not amused.

He would have been still less amused when, after he had sent his creation over the Reichenbach Falls and had thought to see the last of him, he showed up as a specter in Richard Morton's 1894 song "The Ghost of Sherlock Holmes." The refrain gives a flavor of the song:

"Sherlock, Sherlock,"
You can hear the people cry,
"That's the ghost of Sherlock Holmes"
As I go creeping by.
Sinners shake and tremble
Wherever this bogie roams,
And people shout, "He's found us out,
It's the ghost of Sherlock Holmes."

Claude Ralston went further and composed a song, published in 1897 in *The Scottish Students' Song Book*, suggesting that "the Swiss story is a plant," that a lady was involved, and "he'll turn up again, will Sherlock Holmes."

The prescience was worthy of Holmes himself—though Ralston was wrong with his "*cherchez la*

LEFT: A theater poster by the brilliant illustrator Aubrey Beardsley. Like Oscar Wilde, he was a habitué of the Café Royal and a prominent figure in the Aesthetic movement. He died of tuberculosis aged just 25, famed for his erotic and "decadent" work.

femme." For while it was "obvious" to all that Holmes had plunged to his death, we should remind ourselves of his maxim, "There is nothing more deceptive than an obvious fact."

COLOSSUS IN LOVE

Arthur Conan Doyle did not believe that Sherlock Holmes would work on stage. "His reasoning and deductions (which are the whole point of the character) would become an intolerable bore," he said in the early 1890s. As the decade wore on, he began to change his mind—not least because "there are bags of money in it." He penned a five-act drama, which he finished in December 1897 and sent to Herbert Beerbohm Tree, who indicated that he wished to play both Sherlock Holmes and Moriarty— even though some scenes required the two to share the stage. Unwilling to make the changes that Tree urged, Doyle looked elsewhere.

In the end it fell to the American actor William Gillette to write and star in the play, which had the catchy title *Sherlock Holmes.* Doyle wrote to his mother that Gillette had "made a great play out of it, and he is a great actor… I am not usually over sanguine, but I do have great hope for this. It is our trump card." Though Doyle and Gillette had joint credit, Doyle let it be known that the play was Gillette's work. Could he, Gillette wired Doyle to ask, introduce a love interest for Sherlock? "You may marry him, murder him, or do what you like to him," came the reply.

It *was* murder, of a sort: death to the imagination in a way that the printed page was not. Though the play was a hit on Broadway and went on to tour the United States, when it arrived at the Lyceum Theatre in London in September 1901 it garnered mixed reviews.

The restive crowd in the gallery repeatedly called to Gillette to speak up. His low-key performance dissatisfied an audience accustomed to melodrama. *The Times* questioned whether it was politic to bring Sherlock Holmes to the stage at all. "Surely no playhouse is large enough to hold that colossal figure?" And if it was inevitable that Sherlock would find his way into the theater, he at least should not have fallen in love. "We liked to think that he was all head, all triumphant deduction, a walking Euclid." However, he did somewhat redeem the situation, in

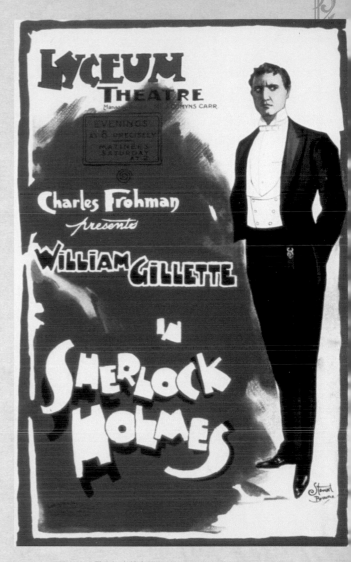

ABOVE: The play *Sherlock Holmes* was written by its star, William Gillette, mixing elements of *A Study in Scarlet, A Scandal in Bohemia,* and *The Adventure of the Final Problem.* Doyle declared himself "charmed both with the play, the acting, and the pecuniary result."

the reviewer's eyes, by "expressing his passion with a stony glare."

Doyle remained optimistic: "*Sherlock* is going to be a *record*, and beat *Charley's Aunt.*" The play did respectably well, closing in London in 1902 after 256 performances—to *Charley's Aunt*'s near 1,500.

CHAPTER 6

Westward Ho

TO KENSINGTON THE GREEN WAY

*"One day in early spring he had so far relaxed as to go for a walk
with me in the Park… For two hours we rambled about together, in silence
for the most part, as befits two men who know each other intimately.
It was nearly five before we were back in Baker Street once more."*

John Watson, *The Adventure of the Yellow Face*

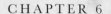

EDGW…

Lancast…
Gate

BAYSW…

Holland
Park

GR.

HOLLAND PARK AVE. NOTTING HILL GT.

Kensington Gardens

Shepherds
Bush

CROSS RTE.

HOLLAND PARK AVE.

18 Stafford Terrace

HOLLAND
PARK

Royal Albert Hall

RD.

HOLLAND RD.

KENSINGTON HIGH ST. KENSINGTON

Kensington
High St

Gloucester
Rd

HAMMERSMITH RD.

WARWICK

Natural History Museum

CROMWELL RD.

A4   W. CROMWELL ROAD

College of Psychic Studies

RD.

OLD BROMPTON RD.

FULHAM PALACE

LILLIE RD.

Earls
Court

FULHAM…

Fulham
Broadway

Brompton Cemetery

DAWES RD.   FULHAM ROAD

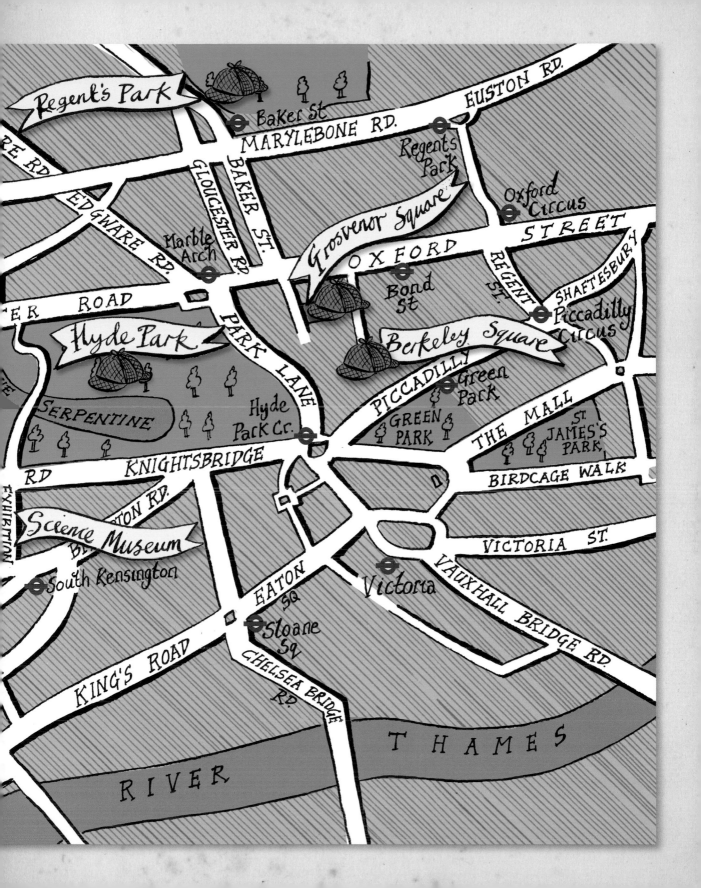

Among its many open spaces, London is blessed with eight Royal Parks. Just minutes north of 221B is **Regent's Park**, with its world-renowned zoo, where the young Arthur Conan Doyle saw the seals kissing their keepers. The world's first scientific zoo was also the first to have a reptile house, built in 1849, where Holmes could make a study of snakes—and, for a change, not of the human kind. He confessed to Watson that Charles Augustus Milverton aroused in him the same "creeping, shrinking sensation" as the serpents in the zoo, "slithery, gliding, venomous creatures, with their deadly eyes and wicked,

flattened faces." Thanks to his zoological researches he was able in an instant to identify the "squat and diamond-shaped head and puffed neck" of the loathsome swamp adder, "the deadliest snake in India," which killed Dr Grimesby Roylott within ten seconds of being bitten, in *The Adventure of the Speckled Band*.

You will find no Indian swamp adder at the London Zoo or any other. The true identify of this vile creature still exercises the minds of herpetologists, who believe that the lethal *Tic polonga*, or Russell's viper, is the prime suspect. It has, at any rate, a diamond-shaped head—but its venom is slow poison and it does not care for swamps. Another conjecture is that Doyle actually *made it up*! That there is *no such* snake! Exclude the impossible and what remains, however improbable, must be the truth.

The zoo was the brainchild of Sir Stamford Raffles, who was the founder of Singapore, and of the Zoological Society of London, of which he was also the first president. Despite his failing health, Raffles dreamed of creating the world's first scientific zoo, for "teaching and elucidating zoology." In 1826 he oversaw the institution of early plans, but died of apoplexy in July of the same year.

The 3rd Marquess of Lansdowne then stepped in, obtaining a lease on a part of the park, where Decimus Burton was appointed to build animal houses. Among Burton's surviving buildings, the earliest is the Clock Tower (1828), which topped off the llamas' hut, but it has been reconstructed since then.

Three Island Pond (1832), ordered by Burton as part of his landscaping, has also since been extended and altered. There, flamingos preen themselves among the weeping willows.

A tall order for Burton, the Giraffe House (1836–7) has 16ft- (5m-) tall doors and still admirably serves its purpose for its lofty inhabitants.

Most famous, though, is the Penguin Pool (1934), designed by the Tecton architectural practice, headed by the Russian émigré Berthold Lubetkin, in a playful Modernist style that was one of the first uses of reinforced concrete. It is a Grade I listed building.

"The Regent's Park" was part of a master design by John Nash for the Prince Regent (the future George IV), which included Regent Street and Carlton House Terrace. The Regent's Canal runs through the park, connecting the Grand

Union Canal to the former London docks. To the north rises Primrose Hill, where Henry VIII once rode to hounds. With its open-air theater, a garden of 12,000 roses, the yellow face of the sun smiling down on the copper beeches, where could be lovelier for a ramble after visiting the Sherlock Holmes Museum?

When Watson says "the Park," however, one takes him to mean **Hyde Park**, across which he would walk from Baker Street to his marital home in Kensington. The eastern boundary of the park is formed by swanky Park Lane, where the Adairs lived in *The Adventure of the Empty House*—"a frequented thoroughfare," now as then. East of Park Lane are **Grosvenor Square**, where Isadora Klein lived in *The Adventure of the Three Gables,* and **Berkeley Square**, home to General de Melville in *The Adventure of the Illustrious Client.*

Grosvenor Square was the traditional home to the official American presence in London. When Dwight D Eisenhower set up a military HQ at No. 20 in World War II, the square acquired the nickname "Eisenhower Platz." Statues of Franklin D Roosevelt, Eisenhower, and Ronald Reagan, which grace the square, are set to be left behind with the US Embassy's move across the river from its 1960s building on the western side of the square.

Berkeley Square, where Winston Churchill lived as a boy, at No. 48, is shaded by some of London's oldest plane trees, planted in 1789. There is a fountain by the Pre-Raphaelite sculptor Alexander Munro, dating from 1865.

Across the main road to the southeast, open spaces continue with Green Park and **St James's Park**, where Charles I was allowed to take a last walk with his pet dog on the morning of his execution. We see the park in the BBC's *Sherlock* in the episode "The Sign of Three," but the bench upon which Holmes and Watson sat, on Birdcage Walk on the south side, across from the Guards Museum, was a prop, and not a public amenity.

ABOVE: Boys fishing in St James's Park, with Buckingham Palace a hazy prospect in the distance. The young Holmes enjoyed a spot of angling in the more bucolic setting of the Norfolk Broads in *The Adventure of the Gloria Scott.*

At the northeastern tip of Hyde Park—where we begin our theoretical amble—are Marble Arch and Speaker's Corner, close to the site of the old Tyburn gallows, a place of public execution until 1783.

From Hyde Park's North Carriage Drive, the West Carriage Drive leads across the Long Water and the Serpentine, the artificial lake that Lestrade dragged in search of the body of Hatty Doran,

the new Lady St Simon, in *The Adventure of the Noble Bachelor*—causing Holmes to scorn, "Have you dragged the basin of Trafalgar Square fountain?" Sir Henry Baskerville came to the park to "look at the folk," a not-unrewarding pastime today.

Hyde Park was another hunting ground for Henry VIII, who confiscated the land from

ABOVE: Londoners get their skates on. The winter of 1890–91 was a bitter, sunless one, with persistent cloud or freezing fog. But with rivers frozen inches deep, there was fun to be had on the ice on the Serpentine in Hyde Park.

Westminster Abbey and enclosed it as a deer chase. Joseph Paxton's Crystal Palace was erected in the park for the Great Exhibition of 1851 before being moved to Sydenham (page 144). The Great Exhibition of the Works of Industry of all Nations, to give it its full title, was organized by the inventor and civil servant Henry Cole, with Prince Albert Francis Charles Augustus Emmanuel of

Saxe-Coburg-Gotha—Queen Victoria's husband.

Much excitement was aroused by the Crystal Palace "monkey closets" in the retiring rooms, the first public lavatories, where a penny bought a clean seat, a towel, a comb, and a shoeshine.

Over centuries, successive monarchs hived off acres of Hyde Park to create Kensington Gardens for Kensington Palace, the birthplace of the future Queen Victoria and now official residence of the Duke and Duchess of Cambridge. Originally a Jacobean mansion, Nottingham House, the palace was created by Sir Christopher Wren, with the necessary extensions and embellishments, for William III. The landscaping of the gardens was ordained by Queen Caroline, wife of George II, from 1728, to designs by Charles Bridgeman. The Round Pond was dug and avenues of trees were planted. The Long Water was created by damming the river Westbourne, a small tributary of the Thames meandering down from Hampstead (page 136). The boundary was marked by a ditch that became known as a ha-ha, perhaps because of the laugh-out-loud reactions it provoked. Anyone respectably attired could use the gardens on a Saturday. Today the ha-ha is filled in; the West Carriage Drive is the notional boundary.

On the south side of Hyde Park is the Albert Memorial, unveiled in 1872 in memory of Victoria's beloved and deeply lamented consort, who had died of typhoid, in 1861, aged just 42. A high-Victorian Gothic Revival extravaganza, the monument was designed by George Gilbert Scott. It was to have "a shrine-like appearance," *Building News* informed its readers, and was "to be enriched to the utmost extent all the arts can go." We can be thankful that the journal was not heeded when it urged making it twice the size. We have here, frankly, quite enough of a good thing.

West of the Long Water is the bronze Peter Pan Statue, designed by Sir George Frampton and commissioned by Doyle's friend and fellow author JM Barrie, creator of the boy who never grew up.

A broad track along the south of the park, Rotten Row, is one of two designated bridleways. The name has nothing to do with the filthy rich— it derives from *Route du Roi*, the King's Road. Horses can be hired from stables nearby for those who want to saddle up. Only remember Holmes's warning in the 2011 film *A Game of Shadows*— "Horses are dangerous at both ends, and crafty in the middle."

ABOVE: Golden memories. George Gilbert Scott's Gothic Revival extravaganza, the Albert Memorial in Kensington Gardens. At the center sits John Henry Foley's gilded statue of Prince Albert shining like a good deed in a naughty world.

Before leaving Kensington Gardens you might have lunch or afternoon tea at The Orangery. Commissioned by Queen Anne in 1704 as a "summer supper house" and place of entertainment, the building was designed by Sir Nicholas Hawksmoor, possibly in collaboration with the Restoration architect and playwright Sir John Vanbrugh, author of the comedy *The Provoked Wife*.

BELOW: Boy wonder. George Frampton's statue, commissioned in 1902, the year that JM Barrie published his first Peter Pan story, in which Peter flew from his nursery to land on this very spot by the Long Water in Kensington Gardens.

If ever there was a wife provoked, then surely it was Mary Watson, née Morstan, that most tractable of women whose husband was forever, with her apparent blessing, gallivanting off on sometimes dangerous missions with a strange man in a deerstalker. Her disappearance from Watson's life and from the canon is one of the great unsolved conundrums. Mary made no more demands upon Watson than did his medical practice, leaving him free to go about playing Boswell to Sherlock's Dr Johnson. So little did Mary see of her husband that, in *The Man with the Twisted Lip*, his name escaped her and she referred to him as "James."

The Watsons' Kensington was very much up and coming, transformed in the latter half of the 19th century from a rural to an urban area, with the building of large terraced houses (row houses) and mansion blocks. There is a constant press of traffic on Kensington High Street, which is lined with fashion stores and restaurants, but it still feels airier here than in the West End. There is a strong French presence, to which Holmes, with his artistic Vernet blood, would have related: you'll find pavement cafés, pâtisseries, and French-language bookshops, and Harding Bros, specialists in busts of Napoleon.

To the east, on Brompton Road in Knightsbridge, is Harrods, the first department store in the world to introduce a moving staircase, in November 1898. It was a conveyer-belt affair with mahogany and plate-glass balustrades. Customers were offered smelling salts or a reviving glass of brandy at the top after nerving themselves to step aboard.

Between the Albert Memorial and South Kensington Underground Station is a quarter nicknamed "Albertopolis," a unique part of London, a kind of theme park of learning and aspiration. Prince Albert was a great enthusiast for improving the minds of the citizenry. Sadly, he was not much appreciated in his lifetime—and is not sufficiently appreciated now.

ECHOES IN THE HALL

Opposite the Albert Memorial we see, first, the **Royal Albert Hall,** where, in *The Adventure of the Retired Colorman*, Holmes escaped from "this weary workaday world by the side door of music" and heard Carina sing. It was to have been called the Central Hall and was intended to promote a deeper appreciation of the arts and sciences—"science," at the time, being broadly interpreted as the pursuit of knowledge in all fields.

The design of the building was inspired by Henry Cole's visits to the ruins of amphitheaters. When it opened in March 1871, "The Royal Albert Hall of Arts and Sciences" was lit by a system of thousands of gas jets that sprang alight within 10 seconds. Electric lighting was installed in 1888—"a very ghastly and unpleasant innovation," as a letter to *The Times* complained. Holmes, visiting in 1898, may or may not have agreed, but more problematic were the acoustics in the elliptical hall—a distinct echo had been evident to all from the Prince of Wales's opening speech. If George Gilbert Scott had had his way, the building would have resembled Ayasofya, the church of Saint Sophia in Constantinople (now Istanbul). It might have been more of a piece with his Albert Memorial. For better or worse he was sidelined.

Press reviews of the new hall were (as ever) not entirely favorable—the *Saturday Review*, for example, called it "a monstrous cross between the Colosseum and a Yorkshire Pie," while *The Examiner* bemoaned "the squat rotundity and Franconish aspect of the music-hall."

The identity of Carina has long exercised the minds of musicologists; no one is sure who he/she was. However, Adelina Patti—daughter of the tenor Salvatore Patti and the soprano Caterina Barilli—certainly sang at the hall over two decades. In Oscar Wilde's *The Picture of Dorian Gray* there is a reference to the soprano and crowd-pleaser—"It is a Patti night and everyone will be there." Could Holmes's

ABOVE: The Royal Albert Hall, where Holmes came to hear Carina sing. Just visible are redbrick, Dutch-gabled mansion blocks—a new design concept for the middle-classes—designed by Richard Norman Shaw in 1879–86 and overlooking Kensington Gardens.

LEFT: Was "Carina" Adelina? The diva Adelina Patti had a colorful love life. She announced her engagement to her third husband at the Royal Albert Hall in November 1898 and gave her official farewell appearance there in 1906.

"Carina" have been a private term of endearment? Carina Adelina? Is there something we've not been told?

If there was some dalliance between the bachelor detective and the thrice-married diva, it was sheer aberration. As he said in *The Sign of Four*, "love is an emotional thing, and whatever is emotional is opposed to that true cold reason which I place above all things. I should never marry myself, lest I bias my judgment."

If time allows, it is certainly worth visiting one or other of South Ken's temples of enlightenment. The **Science Museum** on Exhibition Road has more than 300,000 exhibits, but for fans of *Sherlock*'s Benedict Cumberbatch, the most fascinating exhibit has to be Alan Turing's Pilot ACE computer. Turing, as everyone now knows, was head of code-breaking at Bletchley Park in World War II.

Holmes, one hardly needs to add, had a natural gift for cryptography, being "fairly familiar with all forms of secret writing." In *The Adventure of the Dancing Men*, by frequency analysis he divined that a set of stick men represented letters of the alphabet. He cracked the open-text code in *The Adventure of the Gloria Scott.* Then there were the book codes sent to him by Porlock in *The Valley of Fear.* But most important was his work in World War I when, in *His Last Bow*, he assured Von Bork that he had the replacement naval codes. Probably Turing had read and learned from Holmes's "trifling monograph upon the subject, in which I analyze one hundred and sixty separate ciphers" (*The Adventure of the Dancing Men*). *Possibly* a cocaine syringe in an imitation leather case in the museum's collections was the very one that Sherlock used to inject the drug in seven-per-cent solution.

The **Natural History Museum** to the south, on Cromwell Road, opened in 1881, five years before Doyle first breathed life into Sherlock Holmes. The building, by Alfred Waterhouse, is a glorious work of art in itself, with its German Romanesque facade, spired towers, and terra-cotta. In the cathedral-like space of the Hintze Hall, Dippy the Diplodocus (a plaster-cast model) is, at the time of writing, scheduled to be replaced by the complete skeleton of an 82 foot- (25m-) long blue whale, found beached on the coast of Ireland in 1891. The blue whale skeleton is at present hanging in the Mammals Gallery. Among 80 million specimens, some of the strangest to have come the museum's way are "Archie," a (female) giant squid more than 28 feet (8.6m) long, the blood-chilling giant rat of Sumatra, and the 5 foot- (1.5m-) long fossilized nose of the extinct "chainsaw fish" with its hundreds of sharp teeth.

BONES OF CONTENTION

In 1912 the Natural History Museum's experts were in a fever of excitement. It began in February with a letter from Arthur Charles Dawson, an amateur antiquarian, to Arthur Smith Woodward, the museum's keeper of geology. After some chat about their mutual friend Sir Arthur Conan Doyle (he was at work, said Dawson, on his latest novel, a prehistoric adventure, *The Lost World*), the writer got down to business.

Near the village of Piltdown in East Sussex, he had chanced upon a portion of a human skull. When the paleontologists studied the bone fragments that Dawson had unearthed, they excitedly concluded that they were the remains of a hitherto unknown early hominid, a million-year-old ape-man possessed of a large brain and primitive jawbone and teeth.

This was just about the biggest hoax ever perpetrated on the scientific community. Only in 1953 was "the Piltdown Man," *Eoanthropus dawsoni*, Dawson's dawn man, found to comprise the cranium of a modern human being and the jawbone of an orangutan.

You would think that *someone* at the museum might have smelled a rat. Holmes would not have been taken in. Even without examining the fossils, he would have known that some mischief was afoot, on learning that the bones of elephants, hippopotamuses, rhinos and mastodons, beaver and deer were also found at the site.

Who was behind such skullduggery? Among the suggested perpetrators is Sir Arthur Conan Doyle, a man with a knowledge of anatomy, a collector of fossils who had access to human bones… Was it Doyle's revenge on scientists who scoffed at his Spiritualist sensibilities? Did he, indeed, do it?

RIGHT: A dig at the establishment. Excavations at Piltdown in Sussex unearthed some apparently sensational remains. When Arthur Smith Woodward (vignette, top right), at the Natural History Museum, received a letter from Arthur Charles Dawson (vignette, bottom left), the scientific world was in a ferment.

G FOR THE PILTDOWN MAN

If only we could ask him! Perhaps we should inquire, at our next destination, if they can get hold of him to find out.

With his penchant for true cold reason, Sherlock Holmes would not have had time for the goings-on at **The College of Psychic Studies** (reached by heading south from Cromwell Road on Queen's Gate and turning left onto Queensberry Mews, leading to Queensberry Place, where it is at No. 16). The London Spiritualist Alliance, founded in 1883, bought the building in 1925. At the housewarming party in January 1926, the college president welcoming guests was Sir Arthur Conan Doyle. Healing clinics and consultations in tarot, psychic readings, palmistry, astrology, and more are available today. If distance is a problem, disembodied readings by telephone and Skype can be arranged—how spooky is *that*!

BLESS THIS HOUSE

We cannot say precisely at what address in Kensington Dr and Mrs Watson resided, but we can take a walk to find the very sort of house in which Watson could have been master, enjoying "complete happiness" and "home-centered interests"—a house unchanged since the close of the 19th century. Heading southwest on Kensington High Street, after passing opposite High Street Kensington Underground Station take the third right, Argyll Road, and then the second left, Stafford Terrace. **18 Stafford Terrace**, formerly known as Linley Sambourne House, was the home of the artist Edward Linley Sambourne, a photographer and a political cartoonist for the satirical magazine *Punch*. Sambourne moved to this newly built Italianate terrace house in 1874, upon his marriage to Marion Herapath, a stockbroker's daughter, and it is now a museum open to the public (booking essential for group tours).

This is the real thing, done out in the then-fashionable Aesthetic style. From velvet drapes to William Morris wallpaper, from a Victorian

ABOVE: The empty house. The late-Victorian home of *Punch* cartoonist Edward Linley Sambourne remains just as he left it, cluttered with his possessions and memorabilia. He and his wife, Marion, lived here for 36 years, from 1874.

lavatory to an oak dining table, from porcelain to pictures, it is all exactly as the Sambournes left it. Doyle and Sambourne both contributed to *The Strand Magazine* and they rubbed shoulders at the Reform Club, sitting next to one another at a pre-Christmas dinner in 1892 ("One got drunk," wrote Sambourne in his diary). More than once he played host to Doyle at all-male dinner parties at No. 18. He was in the Lyceum audience to see Gillette play Holmes (page 91), which he noted in his diary without comment. In March 1902 he wrote of going in a four-wheeler after supper to see a "stupid play" titled *Sherlock Jones* at the "wretchedly shabby" Terry's Theatre (the original Coal Hole, page 67).

From High Street Kensington Underground, it is two stops on the District Line to West Brompton and **Brompton Cemetery**, where, in the 2009 Guy Ritchie film *Sherlock Holmes*, Lord Blackwood rose from the family vault. The only cemetery managed by the Royal Parks, it is one of the "Magnificent Seven" Victorian burial parks that ring London, built to relieve the overcrowding in parish graveyards. West Brompton was laid out by Benjamin Baud to the Bruce-Partington Plans and consecrated in 1840. The domed chapel at the center is modeled on the basilica of St Peter's in Rome. Among those buried here are the theater impresario and actor Squire Bancroft, the suffragette Emmeline Pankhurst, Chelsea Football Club founder Charles Augustus Milverton, and the inventor of "self-help" Samuel Smiles. The mother, father, and brother of the composer Arthur Sullivan of Gilbert and Sullivan fame also lie here. Arthur was not, in the event, to join them; at Queen Victoria's insistence his final resting place is St Paul's Cathedral. Less famous names on the burials register include a Mr Nutkins, a Mr McGregor, a Jeremiah Fisher, and one Peter Rabbett. Should you, suspicious reader, suppose that this a spoof, you should know that the children's author Beatrix Potter lived in Bolton Gardens, on Old Brompton Road, from 1866 to 1913. You will look in vain, however, for the graves of a Mrs Tiggy-Winkle, a Miss Moppet, or Tom Kitten.

BELOW: Jude Law and Robert Downey Jr at Brompton Cemetery during filming of the 2009 Guy Ritchie movie *Sherlock Holmes*. As the fiendish Lord Blackwood said in the film when sentenced to hang, "Death… is only the beginning."

OF GHOSTIES AND GHOULIES

Believers, sensitives, skeptics

"But are we to give serious attention to such things? This agency stands flat-footed upon the ground, and there it must remain. The world is big enough for us. No ghosts need apply."

Sherlock Holmes, *The Sussex Vampire*

People have wondered how Arthur Conan Doyle, so fascinated by the occult, was able to create in Sherlock Holmes the ultimate cool rationalist. But, again, that's what fiction writers do—they make things up. It was a mark of Doyle's genius that he created so believable a human being that the question even arises. Holmes's turn of mind also imposed a certain rigor upon plot lines; there could be no recourse to the supernatural.

What is more difficult to square is Doyle's medical scientific background and his absolute faith in the

BELOW LEFT: A good send-off. Notice of a farewell lunch for Sir Arthur Conan Doyle and Lady Doyle at the Holborn Restaurant, given by the Spiritualists of the United Kingdom, before they set off to spread the word in South Africa.

BELOW RIGHT: Gladys Osborne Leonard, described by Doyle as the best trance medium he knew. "[She] sinks into slumber, upon which her voice changes entirely, and what comes through purports to be from her little control, Feda."

OPPOSITE: Elemental, my dear Watson. Doyle appears on film with what seems to be some kind of wraith. He wrote a book making the case for spirit photography—but the camera can lie, as two little girls were to show him with the "Cottingley fairies" prank.

STUDIO CIGARINI

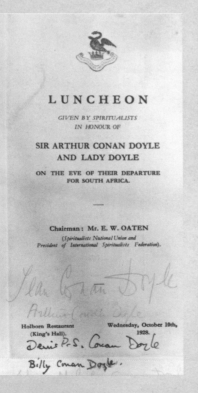

LUNCHEON

GIVEN BY SPIRITUALISTS
IN HONOUR OF

SIR ARTHUR CONAN DOYLE
AND LADY DOYLE

ON THE EVE OF THEIR DEPARTURE
FOR SOUTH AFRICA.

Chairman: Mr. E. W. OATEN
(*Spiritualists National Union and
President of International Spiritualists Federation*).

Holborn Restaurant   Wednesday, October 10th,
(King's Hall).   1928.

paranormal. Even in the late 19th century, when spiritualism enjoyed a vogue, the author risked ridicule for his beliefs. In 1926 he published *The History of Spiritualism* in which he wrote of visiting the trance medium Mrs Osborne Leonard, through whom a little girl named Feda spoke for the waiting spirits on the other side—among them, Doyle's son Kingsley, who, though wounded, had survived the Battle of the Somme, only to die, like so many, of the Spanish influenza in 1918. (The book remains agnostic on the subject of the afterlife, only noting that the skeptic has the disadvantage of never being able to say, "I told you so!")

Trance talking and writing, direct-voice mediumship, ectoplasm, telekinesis, levitation, luminous phenomena, materializations "either of faces, limbs, or of complete figures," all of these, wrote Doyle, "the author has many times seen exhibited to him by the leading mediums of his day."

There was, he continued, "no more curious and dramatic phase of psychic phenomenon than the apport. It is so startling that it is difficult to persuade the skeptic as to its possibility, and even the Spiritualist can hardly credit it, until examples actually come his way." He went on to tell of General Drayson who, through an "apport medium," received

LADIES&GENTS
THESE INNOCENT
LITTLE BIRDS TAKE A
PLANET FROM THE BOX
TELLING YOUR PAST AND
FUTURE LIFE FOR ONE℔

LEFT: Who's a lucky boy, then? An Italian fortune-teller who became a familiar sight on Regent Street. She spoke little English, but no problem! Her "mystical birds from India" would, for a penny, pick out a slip of paper to tell your past and future.

OPPOSITE: Ohio-born Samri (Samuel) Baldwin, magician turned mentalist, toured the world with his show, enthralling millions with his "somnomency," or trance-talking, debunking fake mediums and writing *Spiritualism Exposed*.

"a constant succession of apports of the most curious description—Indian lamps, amulets, fresh fruit, five orange pips…"

For another apport medium, Mr Bailey of Melbourne, Australia, a Hindu-speaking spirit brought a perfect bird's nest containing a single egg, its white shell speckled with brown, which, when broken, contained albumen but no yolk. It came from India, said the courteous spirit when Doyle inquired—the nest and egg of a Jungle sparrow (*Passer pyrrhonotus,* the Sind sparrow).

Among other of Bailey's apports were at least a hundred Assyrian tablets—though when Doyle took one to the British Museum for authentication he was told it was a forgery of a kind made "by certain Jews in a suburb of Baghdad, and, so far as is known, only there." Pondering this he conjectured, "To the transporting agency it is at least possible that the forgery, steeped in recent human magnetism, is more capable of being handled than the original taken from a mound."

All the world's a stage

The cause of mediumship was not served by the many mentalists, mesmerists, and magicians who made a living on the entertainments circuit. In the United States, Samri Baldwin, "The White Mahatma," with his first wife, Clara, and second wife, Kitty, "The Clairvoyant Queen," set out to expose fraudulent spiritualist mediums through their mindreading act. Another American, Washington Irving Bishop, gave "thought-reading" demonstrations but disavowed any supernatural power, explaining that he read thoughts from unconscious body clues.

Very weirdly, Baldwin collapsed and died in the middle of a demonstration in 1889, aged 34, the cause of death given as "hysterocatalepsy," a neurotic disorder characterized by violent emotional episodes and disturbances of sensory motor function.

And what of Black Peter, mentalist and illusionist famous for the cardboard box trick and for causing Lady Frances Carfax to vanish into thin air?

Anyone who wishes to, can read online the two volumes of Doyle's *The History of Spiritualism*—and, indeed, can hear the great man himself (allegedly) speaking through direct-voice medium Leslie Flint about how his career suffered through

his efforts to expound the truth, at leslieflint.com/recordingsdoyle.html

As the schoolboy Arthur Doyle would have heard Hamlet say, "There are more things in heaven and earth, Horatio, than are dreamt of in your philosophy." Or, as Holmes himself put it in *A Case of Identity*, "Life is infinitely stranger than anything which the mind of man could invent."

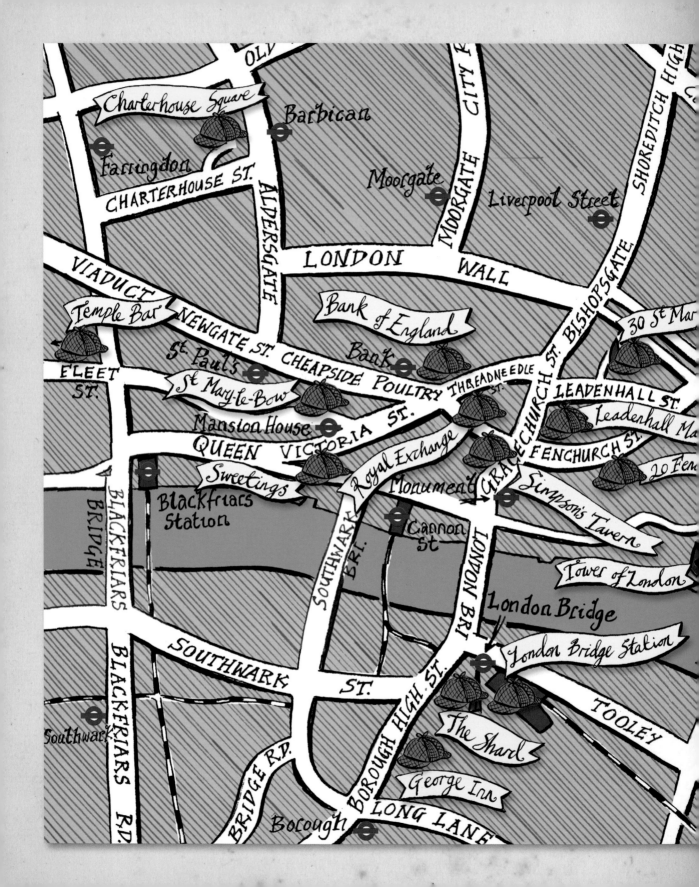

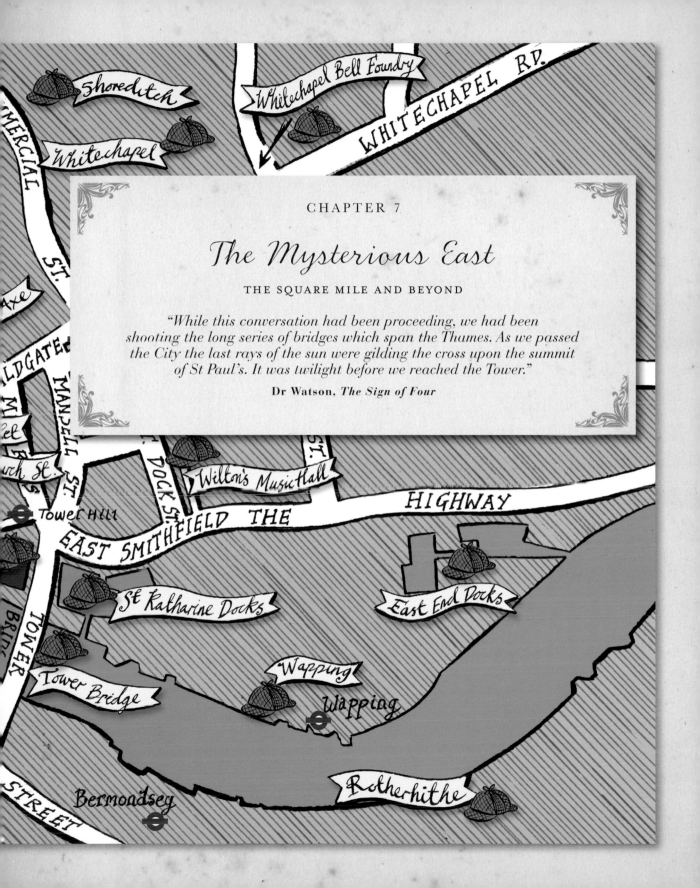

Shoreditch

Whitechapel Bell Foundry

WHITECHAPEL RD.

Whitechapel

COMMERCIAL ST.

AXE

ALDGATE

MANSELL ST.

CHAPTER 7

The Mysterious East

THE SQUARE MILE AND BEYOND

"While this conversation had been proceeding, we had been shooting the long series of bridges which span the Thames. As we passed the City the last rays of the sun were gilding the cross upon the summit of St Paul's. It was twilight before we reached the Tower."

Dr Watson, *The Sign of Four*

Wilton's Music Hall

DOCK ST.

Tower Hill

EAST SMITHFIELD THE HIGHWAY

St Katharine Docks

East End Docks

TOWER BRIDGE

Tower Bridge

Wapping

Wapping

STREET

Bermondsey

Rotherhithe

LUDGATE CIRCUS, LONDON. 7404. G.W.W.

If you walked past the Royal Courts of Justice (page 69) on our Charing Cross-to-St Paul's sortie, you will have noticed in the middle of the road a tall, richly embellished plinth topped by a fearsome winged creature. Often called a griffin, it is in fact a dragon, symbolic of the City of London. You passed at this point from Westminster into the City, the fabled "Square Mile," which is today 1.12 square miles (2.6sq km). Known as the "Temple Bar Memorial," the monument recalls Christopher Wren's Temple Bar, a ceremonial arch and gateway to the City, which stood on the spot for two centuries. In 1878, when the road was widened, it was dismantled and the numbered pieces went into store.

Enter Valerie, Lady Meux (pronounced "Mews"), one-time actress and banjo-playing barmaid, who was married in secret to Sir Henry Meux, a rich brewery-owner ten years her junior. Not that secrecy was Valerie's style—Holmes and Watson doubtless saw her about town, driving herself in a phaeton pulled by zebras. She persuaded her husband to buy Temple Bar, which was rebuilt as an entrance to one of their stately homes, Theobalds Park in Hertfordshire. In 2004 it was returned to London: you can pass through it onto Paternoster Square next to St Paul's Cathedral.

None of the other City gates is still standing. Here be dragons, however—on Victoria Embankment, at Farringdon, Holborn, Blackfriars Bridge, London Bridge, Aldersgate, Aldgate, Bishopsgate, and Moorgate, guarding the City boundaries. They are painted silver, with fiery red tongues, though they are less ferocious than the Temple Bar creature, the work of Charles Bell Birch. The ornate pedestal it sits on is by Horace Jones.

Their investigations took Holmes and Watson many times into the City and the lawless East End, in an age when London was not just the capital of Britain and the cradle of its laws, but the mother city of the Empire and the world's largest

OPPOSITE: Ludgate Circus, at the eastern end of Fleet Street, recalls a gate in the old city wall, named for an ancient King Lud. The King Lud, once a splendid Victorian pub and "home to Welsh rarebit," is today home to a Spanish bank. Turn right toward Blackfriars Bridge to find the Black Friar instead, with its intriguing Arts and Crafts interior.

BELOW: A life of grime. An East End street in the early 1900s is typically overcrowded, dingy, but neighborly. A factory chimney stands tall in the polluted air.

metropolis and financial capital. (Today it vies with New York for that accolade.)

Since then there have been two catastrophic world wars, the Blitz, and, more recently, an apparent invasion from outer space—alien monsters dominate the City skyline. Vanity-driven architectural projects, or works of beauty, depending on your point of view, they rejoice in half-mocking nicknames, such as the Gherkin, the Cheese Grater, the Walkie-Talkie. If you look up you may suppose that the past has been obliterated, and, as we stride out in Holmes's wake, we inevitably find at times that the trail goes cold.

Yet at street level old and new coexist. Of all London, the City was always the scene of the starkest contrasts. Consecrated to mammon, dedicated to civic pomp and ceremony, it was in Holmes's day also inhabited by downtrodden, desperate citizenry, and was notorious for

113

prostitution, debauchery, and vice. The riverside was a warren of dark alleys, of dance halls and doss houses, beer shops and brothels.

Where else but the East End docks would you find the Bar of Gold opium den, where Watson tracked down Isa in *The Man with the Twisted Lip?* He found it on a "vile alley" named "Upper Swandam Lane," behind high wharves to the east of London Bridge, where it lurked between a slop-shop and a gin-shop. Slop-shops sold cheap clothing, run up by sweated labor. Opium could be bought from a chemist without artifice; far

more of it was consumed at home by the bourgeoisie than by dissolute wrecks in low dives. Theatergoers and office workers might knock back a "flash of lightning" in a West End gin palace; the liquor shops of the East End, only, were despicable.

There is no Upper Swandam Lane and the wharves have long gone. If they are to be lamented, squalid riverside London and the East End slums are not. When the social reformer Charles Booth plotted his color-coded "poverty maps," he began, in 1886, with the East End. His

BELOW: A stereotypical depiction of an East End Chinese opium den. Certainly Chinese immigrants smoked opium—in their homes, and in somewhat ad hoc social clubs—but the image of dissolution and degradation was promoted by moral campaigners.

ABOVE: Charles Booth's map of Shoreditch in the East End. The clusters of red around Shoreditch High Street, the main north–south artery, denote well-to-do homes, but dark blue signifies "very poor, casual [labor], chronic want", and black the "lowest class, vicious, semi-criminal."

street plan of Shoreditch, for example, shows a moderate red presence, denoting lower-middle-class, hardworking, sober shopkeepers and the like. But there are large pockets of black, which Booth explained referred to "The lowest class… occasional laborers, street sellers, loafers, criminals and semi-criminals. Their life is the life of savages, with vicissitudes of extreme hardship and their only luxury is drink." There are areas, too, of dark blue: "Casual earnings, very poor. The labourers do not get as much as three days' work a week… Class B is not one in which men are born and live and die so much as a deposit of those who from

mental, moral and physical reasons are incapable of better."

In this chapter we make a brief excursion outside the City bounds, before embarking on a great swoop through and around the city's heart, finally ending south of the river. We would not dream of trudging all the way. This is a *notional* walk, a round-up, from which to pick and choose. And we have to be relaxed about the march of progress. As Sherlock said in *A Study in Scarlet*, "There is nothing new under the sun. It has all been done before," so London will go on reinventing itself *ad infinitum*.

SAXE-COBURG—WHERE?

In *The Red-Headed League* Holmes and Watson took the Underground to Aldersgate and walked a short way to Saxe-Coburg Square. Aldersgate Street Station, renamed Barbican, is where we alight. The prime contender for Saxe-Coburg Square is **Charterhouse Square**, just outside the City. It does not match Watson's description of "a poky, little, shabby-genteel place," but there was something of that back then. The west side had been pulled down and turned over to commercial premises, including a five-story warehouse. The electrical engineers Ferranti's had set up shop there. The south side had been partially demolished, the remainder given over to warehouses, milliners, the rag trade, a knitting-machine maker, staff hostels, a showroom for oriental carpets, and, at the sign of three gilt balls, the shop of the shock-headed pawn broker Jabez Wilson.

Formerly middle-class, the square was in decline as a residential enclave—think weedy grass, faded laurels, and a smoke-laden, uncongenial atmosphere. The 1930s Art Deco Florin Court on the east side was to replace late 17th-century houses that Watson might have noticed. (The apartment block will be familiar to fans of another great detective, having featured as Whitehaven Mansions, home to Hercule Poirot in ITV's long-running series.)

"You *see*, but you do not observe," Sherlock had occasion to admonish his sidekick. So it was that Watson failed to observe, on the north side, this square's defining glory, a former 14th-century Carthusian monastery, with the house built for the Charterhouse physician in 1716, over the medieval gateway. Seized in 1537 in Henry VIII's Dissolution, it became a swanky private mansion, then a school for boys (which moved to Surrey in 1872), and an almshouse for gentlemen—which it remains to this day (the Charterhouse Almshouse, tours are available but must be booked in advance via the website, www.thecharterhouse.org.)

BELLS, BOURSE, AND BANK

From St Paul's Cathedral, we might set off down Cheapside, which, with Poultry and then Cornhill, forms the main west–east thoroughfare. Robert Ferguson would have walked down Cheapside on the way to his solicitors at Old Jewry in *The Adventure of the Sussex Vampire*, passing Wood Street, Bread Street, Milk Street, Honey Lane, Ironmonger Lane…

On the right is **St Mary-le-Bow**. The church bells belabor the air with metallic peels, and only those born within earshot of "Bow bells" can claim to be true cockneys, those East End natives with their ingenious rhyming slang. And now—would you Adam 'n' Eve it?—the clangor that, in Holmes's day, reverberated right across the river to Southwark, to the north as far as Waltham Forest, and over Tower Hamlets to the east, is so drowned out by noise pollution that its reach has dwindled to a few streets. The cockney heritage is all but brown bread. It's enough to make you want to slink off to the rub-a-dub and get elephant's trunk!

It was these bells that called the mercer Dick Whittington back from Highgate: "Turn again, Whittington, Lord Mayor of London." Or not exactly, for that was in the 14th century. The original church was consumed by the Great Fire of 1666 and rebuilt by Wren on the model of the Basilica of Maxentius in Rome. The name derives from bowed arches in the 11th-century crypt. Descend the stairs for lunch in the Café Below—so much more atmospheric than One New Change, next door, with its fashion shops, bars, and restaurants.

Beyond St Mary-le-Bow, turn right down Queen Victoria Street to find **Sweetings**, a Victorian survivor at No. 39. Sherlock Holmes had oysters on the brain in *The Adventure of the Dying Detective* when he murmured that he could not think why the whole bed of the ocean was not one solid mass of them, so prolific the creatures seemed—"Ah, I am wandering! Strange how the brain controls the brain!" Perhaps he was more a turtle-soup man;

ABOVE· Victorian Cheapside has been much redeveloped, but you can still see John Bennett's clock shop frontage, with its clock, dragon weather vane, and figures of Gog and Magog—just go to Greenfield Village, Dearborn, Michigan, where Henry Ford replanted it in 1931.

both were on offer at this fish restaurant, opened in 1889. Samuel Butler, Victorian novelist and iconoclast, describes in *Ramblings in Fleet Street* how he "saw some turtles in Mr Sweeting's window and was tempted to stay and look at them." Had he had but a half a crown he might have bought one to eat, the better to comprehend it. In John Galsworthy's *The Forsyte Saga*, Soames Forsyte lunched at the "celebrated eating house,"

taking his smoked salmon and a glass of Chablis standing up, "finding the position beneficial for his liver." Sweetings opens only for lunch and does not take bookings. You eat in the bar, or club-style in the dining room with its mosaic floor, where a prawn cocktail is served without any hint of postmodern irony.

Queen Victoria Street leads up to Bank, where one is confronted by the portico of William Tite's

Royal Exchange, based on the Pantheon in Rome and opened in 1844. The original exchange building was commissioned by a merchant, Sir Thomas Gresham, in 1563, to rival Antwerp's bourse, and became very fashionable after a visit by Elizabeth I. However, it, too, went up in smoke in the Great Fire. A second building burned down in January 1838, its chiming clock gamely ringing out "Life Let us Cherish," "God Save the Queen," and, finally, "There's Nae Luck Aboot the Hoose." An overheated stove in Lloyd's Coffee House was the likely culprit for the blaze.

For nearly 150 years the Royal Exchange was the home of the Lloyd's of London insurance market (now relocated to the distinctive Lloyd's building on Lime Street). Within the Royal Exchange, an open court, reminiscent of the inner courtyard of an Italian palazzo, is occupied by the Grand Café and surrounded by smart boutiques—much as Gresham intended.

To the left of the Royal Exchange is Threadneedle Street and, on it, the **Bank of England,** responsible for issuing the nation's bank notes so brilliantly faked by the Chicago forger Rodger Presbury in *The Adventure of the Three Garridebs.* The bank—with 4,600 tons of gold in its bombproof vault—is held to be impregnable. To the master criminal Moriarty such a challenge was irresistible. In the BBC *Sherlock* episode "The Reichenbach Fall," he opened the Bank vault at the same moment as he broke into the Crown Jewels case and unlocked the cells at Pentonville Prison with his cellphone.

Counterfeiters rob by shadier means. In the 1946 movie *Dressed to Kill* (entitled *Sherlock Holmes and the Secret Code* in the UK), Basil Rathbone's Holmes was in a race to recover the Bank of England's printing plates for £5 notes, against the ruthless gang-leader Mrs Hilda Courtney. Courtney had a real-life precedent. In August 1873, four Americans—George Bidwell and his brother Austin, George Macdonnell, and Edwin Noyes Hills—were indicted at the Old Bailey "for felonious forgery of Bills of Exchange for

£100,000 with intent to defraud the Governor and Company of the Bank of England." From the dock, the Harvard-educated Macdonnell delivered an utterance worthy of Sherlock Holmes himself: "Forgery is a very wretched, unhappy, miserable and contemptible art, [but] it is an art nonetheless." Sentence: penal servitude for life.

The Bank again became a crime scene in 1925—indeed, was subject to what Nikolaus Pevsner called "the greatest architectural crime, in the City of London, of the 20th century." The victim was Sir John Soane, the Greek interpreter, arch exponent of the Neoclassical style, who spent 45 years, until his retirement in 1833, altering, enlarging, and refining the Bank—a building begun by George Sampson in the 1730s and expanded by Robert Taylor in 1765–88. It was, Soane said, "the pride and boast" of his life.

They destroyed Soane's three-story treasure when it was no longer fit for purpose. What we have now is Herbert Baker's stone-clad, steel-framed rebuild, within Soane's curtain wall; rising to seven stories, it has three more floors below ground. Sculpted figures are by Charles Wheeler, including the Lady of the Bank in the pediment (replacing a statue of Britannia that had given rise to the Bank's nickname "the Old Lady of Threadneedle Street"). "Miss Threadneedle Street is wearing a permanent wave," sneered the *Evening Standard*, "and not a great deal else… She is dandling on her knee what looks like a small Greek temple… or again it may be a toy savings bank." On the north side on the corner of Lothbury is a statue of Sir John Soane by William Reid Dick. A museum is devoted to the Bank's history, and four times a year group guided tours are offered. They are said to be well worth taking, but be prepared to wait in line—and don't expect a goody bag.

To the right of the Royal Exchange is Cornhill, lined with some handsome classical buildings. There are two Wren churches—St Michael's Cornhill, completed by Nicholas Hawksmoor, with a porch by George Gilbert Scott, and St Peter-

ABOVE: Oyez! Oyez! Oyez! Traditionally, Royal Proclamations such as the dissolution of Parliament are read out by the Common Crier, accompanied by the Serjeant at Arms for the City of London, from the steps of the Royal Exchange.

upon-Cornhill. The building next door was designed in 1893 by the architect Ernest Runtz, architect of the Gaiety Theatre, and its Doulton terra-cotta facade has some curious adornments: three malevolent red devils by WJ Neatby, one spitting, one giving the finger, all casting down curses on a rector who complained that the new building encroached by one foot on church land.

Between Cornhill and Lombard Street is a labyrinth of medieval courts and alleyways. Before

St Michael's Cornhill church, on Ball Court, is Simpson's Tavern, London's oldest chophouse, founded in 1757—though women would have to wait until 1916 to be admitted. And on St Michael's Alley is the Jamaica Wine House, catering to the City stalwarts, the loss adjustor, the bank teller, the stockbroker's clerk. The present building dates from 1869, but the Jamaica Wine House began life as London's first coffee house. It was opened in 1652 by Pasqua Rosee from

ABOVE: Founded in 1757 by Thomas Simpson, "London's oldest chophouse" is approached via a narrow alley. In a dining room fitted with 19th-century stall seating, its "bill of fare" includes such staples as Lancashire hotpot and steak-and-ale pie.

Smyrna, Western Turkey, who had arrived in London as a servant of a merchant, Daniel Edwards. The diarist Samuel Pepys was among those who flocked to drink the exotic brew. Shepherd Neame, who run it as a public house, boast that they are London's oldest brewers, founded in 1698. Imbibe a glass of Bishops Finger along with the history and brace up as we fast-forward to the 21st century.

TALL TALES OF THE CITY

At the eastern end of Cornhill, Bishopsgate leads north, reminding us how, in *The Sign of Four*, Inspector Athelney Jones confessed to Holmes, "I'll never forget how you lectured us all on causes and inferences and effects in the Bishopsgate jewel case." There is no sense of Sherlock Holmes to be had there.

You won't find a flavor of Holmes on Leadenhall Street either, which runs straight ahead from Cornhill. This is where Hosmer Angel claimed to work as a cashier in an office in *A Case of Identity*, and Mary Sutherland addressed her letters to him at the post office. Nor is there so much as a whisper of Holmes's London on Fenchurch Street, to the south—where Westhouse and Marbank was located in the same sorry tale.

Holmes and Watson would have recognized Fenchurch Street Station—the first train station built within the City—but not Rafael Viñoly's 20 Fenchurch Street building. Initially nicknamed the "Walkie-Talkie" because of its shape, it was soon dubbed "The Walkie-Scorchie" after the strange case of the melting cars and smoking doormat. The mystery was solved through the realization that the building's concave shape was causing the large windows to reflect an intense beam of sunlight onto the road, leading to the apparently preternatural "death ray" effect. Investigators will surely have consulted that indispensable modern classic *The Dynamics of Combustion* by ML Holmes—mother to Gattis's Mycroft and Cumberbatch's Sherlock in the BBC series.

At its southern end, Bishopsgate continues as Gracechurch Street, where you will find the main entrance to **Leadenhall Market**. The market dates back to the 14th century, though it was redesigned in 1881 by Horace Jones (who designed the Temple Bar memorial that was our introduction to the City) and redecorated in 1990–91. Perfumer and pizzeria have replaced poulterers, but the beautiful market building with its glass roof and cobbled floors is as Victorian as you please. You may have seen it in *Harry Potter and the Mazarin Stone* when it was en route to the Leaky Cauldron wizarding pub and Diagon Alley.

East of the market, beyond the confluence of Leadenhall Street and Fenchurch Street, is Aldgate. Here we are sobered by the memory that, in *The Adventure of the Bruce-Partington Plans*, the body of Arthur Cadogan West was found by a plate-layer named Mason at the Underground station, lying by the tracks, his head crushed— and *without a ticket*! Under the bylaws, a £2 fine was to be levied from anyone traveling on the train roof. Useless, however, to ask Cadogan West to pay up and look pleasant! He was already dead when his body was dumped on the roof of a train in Kensington, to be shaken off by points here.

East of Aldgate is Whitechapel, where, to the despair of the locals, under cover of darkness, a dreadful menace stalks the streets: Jack the Ripper tours, fifty strong, are a nightly occurrence. One resident, driven to distraction, turned a hose on a tour guide from an upper balcony.

Go in daylight, on a weekday, to visit Britain's oldest manufacturing company, the **Whitechapel Bell Foundry** (32–4 Whitechapel Road), established in 1570. Museum displays can be seen in the foyer of the building, which dates from 1670 when it was a coaching inn, and pre-booked foundry tours are available at a price, subject to caveats about safety.

Among the significant bells cast here are Big Ben (1858, page 44), the Liberty Bell (1752), the bells of St Michael's, Charleston, South Carolina (1764), the Great Bell of Montreal (1843), the bells of St Mary-le-Bow (1738, 1762, 1881, and 1956, page 116) and of St Clement Danes (1588) of "Oranges and Lemons" fame,

and, not least, the chimer at St Mary Abbots, Kensington (1853). Its great church clock, with its measured beats, seemed to sound the dirge of hopes for Sherlock and Mycroft, Watson and Inspector Lestrade, as they waited in Oberstein's empty house in *The Adventure of the Bruce-Partington Plans*.

Going back to Aldgate, take a left on the Minories, passing Starbucks, William Hill bookmakers, One Stop Food and Wine, and

RIGHT: At the heart of old Roman London, beautiful Leadenhall Market, with its cobbled floors and green, maroon, and cream paintwork, dates from the Middle Ages but was redesigned in Victorian times by Sir Horace Jones—architect, also, of the old Billingsgate fish market and Smithfield meat market.

Straubenzee's workshop. Take another left, down Shorter Street onto Royal Mint Street. Just after it becomes Cable Street, turn right on Ensign Street, and left on Graces Alley, to **Wilton's Music Hall**, the oldest surviving music hall in the world.

During the second half of the 19th century, music halls offered entertainment to the masses: happy, bawdy, sing-along entertainments, with a humor stiff with innuendo. Stars included the male impersonator Vesta Tilley, the comic and frequent pantomime dame Dan Leno, and Marie Lloyd, past mistress of the toothy grin, knowing wink, and proverbial dig in the ribs. Wilton's, being out of the way, is a rather well-kept secret, a mid-19th-century music hall attached to three 18th-century terrace houses and a pub. In 1888 it became a Methodist mission, and during the dock strike of 1889, soup was dispensed from the Mahogany Bar. Today it once again offers a varied program of entertainments, and the restored but still highly atmospheric rooms are a great place for a drink. You have probably already seen it—as the gentleman's club in *A Game of Shadows*.

Ensign Street leads down to The Highway, Wapping, where a right turn takes you to the entrance gateway to St Katharine Docks. Designed and built by Thomas Telford after 1825, the docks were created with the sweeping away of over a thousand slum houses in such mean streets as Pillory Lane, Cat's Hole, and Dark Entry. In its

BELOW: Champagne Charlies. Jude Law and Robert Downey Jr in *A Game of Shadows*, when Watson's stag night didn't go quite to his plan. The filming location was Wilton's, the world's oldest surviving music hall, with its distinctive "barley-sugar" iron pillars supporting the gallery.

ABOVE: A bridge too far? The grand opening of Tower Bridge by the Prince of Wales in June 1894. The critic for the *Pall Mall Gazette* deplored "a subtle quality of ungainliness, a certain variegated ugliness… It is excellently situated for our ugliest public work."

heyday St Katharine Docks handled such exotic cargoes as rum, sugar, teas, oriental spices, indigo, marble, brandy, and wine. Today leisure boats lie at anchor, and chain restaurants serve formulaic food. *Sic transit gloria mundi.*

Steps lead up to another of London's most iconic landmarks, **Tower Bridge**, the work of Horace Jones (again!) and John Wolfe Barry, youngest son of Sir Charles. Built of Cornish granite and Portland stone, and incorporating 11,000 tons of steel, with its two towers and twin "bascules" (French for "see-saws," working on a

drawbridge principle), it is probably the most famous bascule and suspension bridge in the world. Eight years in the building, it cost £1,184,000 and the lives of ten workmen.

It was opened with much fanfare by the Prince and Princess of Wales on June 30, 1894, with *The Times* hailing it as "one of the great engineering achievements of the Victorian age." However, the curmudgeons of much of the press welcomed the bridge with about as much enthusiasm as modern-day Londoners greeted St Mary Axe ("the Gherkin") in 2003–4—before learning to love it and voting it London's favorite tower. In December 1884 the architecture critic of the *Pall Mall Gazette* bemoaned a "horrible mixture of iron work and gothic stonework… This huge but childish structure shows the vanity of forty years of sentimental gush about art." He detested its "lack of proportion, its niggled and meaningless ornamentation." There is no pleasing some people.

Before Tower Bridge opened, to transit the river at this point one had to go by boat or use the Tower Subway beneath the Thames. Some 20,000 people a day paid the halfpenny toll to use this ill-lit iron intestine. There was, obviously, not much headroom: Charles Dickens Jr counseled, "It is not advisable for any but the very briefest of Her Majesty's lieges to attempt the passage in high-heeled boots, or with a hat to which he attaches any particular value." With the new option to cross Tower Bridge for free, on foot or by vehicle, the populace saw no contest, and the subway went out of business in 1898. On Tower Hill, blinkered Londoners see, but so often do not *observe*, a smallish brick rotunda that was once an entrance kiosk to the subway. Today the tunnel is a useful conduit for TV cables.

Across the river, on the south side of the bridge, is Bermondsey, with the historic cobbled street known as Shad Thames, and Butler's Wharf, a kind of Conranopolis created by the restaurateur Sir Terence Conran, who, in 1983, acquired an 11-acre (4.5ha) site and 23 derelict Victorian warehouses with the intention of creating a "gastrodome." The restaurants were bought by D&D London in 2006. Riverside dining offers matchless views of that "huge, childish structure" we so love.

Downriver on the south side is **Rotherhithe,** once part of the thriving Surrey Commercial Docks. Holmes was working on a case there in *The Adventure of the Dying Detective*, and returned to Baker Street, seemingly mortally ill, to take to his bed.

The Pilgrim Fathers set sail for America from Rotherhithe, via Plymouth, Devon, aboard the *Mayflower* in 1620. The ship's captain Christopher Jones is buried in an unmarked grave at St Mary's. Beside the church is the oak-beamed Mayflower public house (117 Rotherhithe Street). It has its own jetty, a "snug" of built-in wooden settles, and a license to sell both British and US postage stamps, having functioned as a post office for the river. Another mystery: what use are US postage stamps in London?

Returning north, we may find that our way across Tower Bridge is obstructed. Tourists love to see the bascules raised to let tall ships through, but to Londoners anxious to get to work on the opposite bank, the novelty of seeing a great slab of road rearing up can wear thin.

It was opposite the ancient citadel the **Tower of London** that the police launch intercepted the *Aurora* in *The Sign of Four*. The White Tower, the cold stone heart of the Tower of London, is Norman, built by William the Conqueror to oppress and subdue the natives. Dating from 1098 and standing 89 feet (27m) tall, it was not surpassed in height until 1310 with the completion of the old St Paul's Cathedral.

If the White Tower seems ancient, at All Hallows by the Tower, the City's oldest church, founded in 675, there is a surviving 7th-century arch from the Saxon church—and in the crypt beneath is a 2nd-century Roman pavement. Samuel Pepys watched London burn in 1666 from the church's tower. Having been restored in the late 19th century, All Hallows was severely damaged during World War II and was rebuilt, and rededicated in 1957.

From 200 AD London's Roman wall stretched for 2 miles (3.2m) around the City, starting at Tower Hill and ending at Blackfriars. Today chunks of the wall may be seen at various vantage points. If you head up Cooper's Row from Tower Hill, you will find—in the courtyard of the Grange City Hotel—a large section of the wall. The lower portion, up to about 13 feet (4m), is Roman, with medieval additions above.

Going back down toward the river and heading

ABOVE: Tall order. Rafael Viñoly's 20 Fenchurch Street, nicknamed the "Walkie-Talkie," was built to a scaled-down plan after concerns about its visual impact on the ancient Tower of London (pictured) and St Paul's Cathedral. Heritage groups are not appeased.

west on Lower Thames Street, you pass the Custom House, where customs duties were first paid as long ago as the 14th century; the present building, by David Laing, dates from the early 19th century. Just beyond it is the old Billingsgate Fish Market, once the largest fish market in the world; the present, arcaded building dates from 1875 and is by Horace Jones, yet again. When the fish market was relocated to east London, the building was refurbished and is now a "hospitality and events space."

The next crossing is London Bridge. Its previous incarnation, built in 1825–31, was likely the "broad balustraded bridge" that Holmes and Watson went hammering over, with the murky river flowing sluggishly beneath, in *The Man with the Twisted Lip*. That Victorian bridge was sold in 1968 to a Missouri entrepreneur, who reassembled it in Arizona, and the present London Bridge was opened in 1973. The Victorian bridge's predecessor, medieval London Bridge, was completed in 1209, in the reign of King John, six

years before he set his seal to Magna Carta. It was lined with shops and houses, and enlivened from time to time by the spectacle of spikes skewering the severed heads of traitors who met their end at the Tower. The medieval bridge was demolished after the Victorian replacement opened. The Church of St Magnus the Martyr, a little downstream from the present London Bridge, incorporates the old pedestrian entrance to the medieval bridge.

London Bridge Station, on the south side of the river, saw a lot of traffic, with Holmes et al embarking for Woolwich in *The Adventure of the Bruce-Partington Plans* and for Beckenham in *The Adventure of the Greek Interpreter*. Holmes and Watson boarded the train for Blackheath here in *The Adventure of the Retired Colorman*, while John Hector McFarlane arrived there from Norwood in *The Adventure of the Norwood Builder* and was trailed to Baker Street by the police.

LEFT: Steamers and open barges crowd Fish Wharf, Billingsgate, in the Pool of London. Horace Jones's arcaded market hall was built in 1875 to house the world's largest dedicated fish market. Every day at 5am a frenzy of trading would begin.

ABOVE: A galleried coaching inn, The George dates from the 17th century and is the last of its kind in London. No doubt cabbie and Borough resident John Clayton (in *The Hound of the Baskervilles*) would stop in for an ale—although not, of course, when he was driving.

Today, what you see—*all* you see, so much does it insist upon it—is Renzo Piano's glass-clad pyramid the Shard—at the time of writing, the tallest building in the European Union.

The area is Borough, or "The Borough," where lived John Clayton, the cabbie who drove Stapleton around in *The Hound of the Baskervilles*. Borough Market, across from London Bridge Station, with a thousand years of history, has in recent times become a top foodie destination.

In the Floral Hall on Stoney Street is Brindisa, who supply the tapas so enjoyed by Holmes and Watson in *Sherlock* (page 83).

At 77 Borough High Street is the **George Inn**, London's last galleried coaching inn, which dates from the 17th century. So what's it to be? Chorizo from Brindisa's grill, in ciabatta with piquillo peppers and salad, or a pint of Old Speckled Hen and a little something at the George Inn? If you've come this far you deserve it!

RINGING THE CHANGES

Communications and Travel

"I then shouted into M the following sentence: 'Mr Watson—come here—I want to see you.' To my delight he came and declared that he had heard and understood what I said."

This was not about Holmes summoning his friend in a more than usually peremptory manner, but Alexander Graham Bell, recording in his laboratory notebook on March 10, 1876, how he made the world's first telephone call. He bawled into the mouthpiece of his new invention, and his assistant, Thomas Watson, duly appeared. Asked to repeat the words he had heard, Watson did so. "We then changed places," Bell related, "and I listened at S [speaker] while Mr Watson read a few passages from a book into the M. It was certainly the case that articulate sounds proceeded from S. The effect was loud but indistinct and muffled."

Whether or not Bell indeed invented the telephone independently of Elisha Gray, who was working on a similar device, or, indeed, *stole* Gray's ideas and bribed an alcoholic patent officer as some people claim, is the kind of poser Sherlock would have relished. Bell's application reached the US patent office in Washington DC on February 14, 1876, just hours before or *after* Gray submitted his own caveat, depending on who you believe.

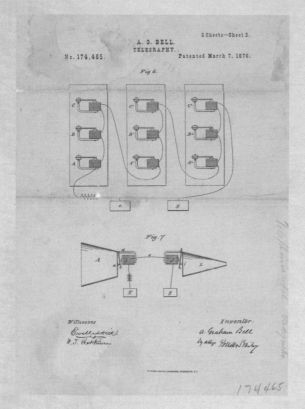

Preece, president of the Society of Telegraph Engineers, proved himself less than visionary when he responded to the question of whether the telephone was the way of the future: "I think not." It was different over in America, he reasoned. "Here we have a superabundance of messengers, errand boys, and things of that kind."

So we did—not least the "Baker Street Irregulars," street urchins such as Wiggins, who, for a silver shilling, could be dispatched on errands all over town, fleet and agile, knowing all the back ways, able to dodge through the crowds. Still, Preece was very wrong. There was even to be a phone at Baker Street. By the time of *The Adventure of the Retired Colorman,* Holmes was able to declare, "Thanks to the telephone and the help of the Yard, I can usually get my essentials without leaving this room."

OPPOSITE: Experimental, my dear Watson. Alexander Graham Bell with his prototype telephone. Bell was born in Doyle's native Edinburgh. He moved to the USA, where he pioneered a system of "visible speech" devised by his father, to teach deaf children, before founding a school in Boston to train teachers of the deaf. In 1873 he became professor of vocal physiology at Boston University.

ABOVE LEFT: Wrong number? Bell's patent-application drawing and oath. The patent was granted on March 7, 1876, although there is dispute as to who should take the credit for the invention..

BELOW: Street smart. Holmes would use those wily urchins the Baker Street Irregulars as informants and emissaries. Often the quickest way to deliver a message was to slip a boy a shilling to run the errand.

When we first met Sherlock he had occasional resort to the telegraph office, wiring Watson in *The Boscombe Valley Mystery,* "Have you a couple of days to spare?" In *The Adventure of the Norwood Builder,* he received a telegram from Inspector Lestrade on the matter of McFarlane's guilt—his "little cock-a-doodle of victory." Again, it was by telegram that Lestrade, the professional, summoned Sherlock Holmes, the amateur, to 131 Pitt Street, Kensington, in *The Adventure of the Six Napoleons.*

The telegram was a swift method of communication, but the telephone was set to trump it. In 1879 exchanges opened on Leadenhall Street in the City and Palace Chambers in Westminster, to serve 200 subscribers. In September of that year Edison's opened an exchange on Queen Victoria Street (page 116), with two more following in early 1880, serving 172 subscribers.

Although he would conceive the idea of wireless telegraphy four years later, and in 1877 had been the first to import Bell telephones to the UK, William

BOX CLEVER

Still, the art of letter writing was far from dead and the mail was a model of speed and efficiency. Collections and deliveries were admirably frequent, with boxes emptied from 6.30am—so it was that, in *The Adventure of the Copper Beeches*, Holmes could receive before breakfast a note penned to him by Violet Hunter dated the night before. Such speed is undreamed of today.

The burgeoning rail system meant that mail could be whizzed around the country, where in the past it had been carried by stagecoach. The British postal service had its origins in Tudor times, when Brian Tuke was appointed Master of the Posts by Henry VIII and set up a network of postmasters across the country. Charles I opened the service to the public, and Charles II established the General Post Office in the year of the Restoration of the monarchy, 1660.

The first pillar boxes, which were not a standard color, appeared on Jersey in the Channel Islands, in 1852, at the suggestion of Anthony Trollope, who held senior rank within the Post Office before becoming a successful novelist. When the scheme proved a success, pillar boxes were installed on the mainland in 1853—with London getting its first five in 1855: on Piccadilly, Pall Mall, the Strand, Fleet Street, and Rutland Gate in Kensington. Some ornate early pillar boxes had one design flaw: the aperture for the letters was missing. On another design the royal cipher, the crown, and the words "Post Office" had accidentally been left off.

The boxes afforded not just convenience but a new privacy for correspondents, who no longer had to present themselves at a post office, letter in hand, or to trust an envelope to an emissary. For women in particular this was a blessing, although some were as distrustful of the grinning "iron stumps" as the fictitious Miss Stanbury who "had not the faintest belief that any letter put into one of them would ever reach its destination." Miss Stanbury appears in the 1869 novel *He Knew He was Right*—its author, Anthony Trollope, was having a laugh, but Miss S may have had a point. In 2001 a postcard finally arrived in Aberdeen, posted from Australia in 1889 and lost for 112 years in the system.

In the tales of Sherlock Holmes, many a missive found its way into one of the cylindrical red pillar boxes that appeared in 1879 and have not greatly changed since. The more visible scarlet replaced the dull green

ABOVE: Arthur Conan Doyle was a prolific letter-writer, corresponding in particular with his mother, Mary. He was at sea, bound for Australia, in December 1920, when she died of a stroke. She had "neither sympathy nor understanding" for his spiritualism. "She understands now," he would conclude.

OPPOSITE: The late-Victorian mail system would put today's to shame. In London there were as many as 12 deliveries a day, hourly between 7.30am and 7.30pm, and a letter dropped in a postbox could land on the addressee's doormat within a couple of hours.

color that had been introduced in 1859, because people kept bumping into the old-style boxes in low light. If you happen to be in Cornwall Gardens, Kensington, you can drop a postcard into a hexagonal Penfold-style pillar box introduced in 1866, though you will have to go to Eton, Berkshire, to find on the High Street a fluted Doric-style column with a vertical slot, from an 1856 design. The British Postal Museum has a model from the brief reign of Edward VIII, close to the Mail Centre at the misleadingly named "Mount Pleasant."

No. 660.]   7th Mo. (JULY), 1888.   [Price 6d. By Post, 9d.

OFFICIALLY  EVERY MONTH.

Under the Patronage of HER MAJESTY THE QUEEN,
H. R. H. The Prince of Wales, the Royal Family, both Houses of Parliament,
all the Government Offices, Banks, and other Public Offices, &c., &c.

BRADSHAW'S
GENERAL RAILWAY AND STEAM NAVIGATION
GUIDE,
FOR GREAT BRITAIN AND IRELAND,

Containing the Official Time Tables, specially arranged, of all the Railways in
ENGLAND, WALES, SCOTLAND, AND IRELAND.

KEY TO THE GENERAL ARRANGEMENT AND PLAN OF THE GUIDE, see page xiii.

TABLE OF CONTENTS, with Official names of Railways........pages xiv to xvii.
STEAM PACKET ADVERTISEMENTS and Sailings of Steamers..pages 410 to 480.
HOTEL AND HYDROPATHIC ADVERTISEMENTS.............pages 485 to 616.
BRADSHAW'S RAILWAY GUIDE INDICATOR ....see back of Map.
ALMANACK and TIDE TABLE, page vi. | TELEGRAPH OFFICES, see Index.
The FIGURES on the MAP refer to the PAGE where the TRAIN SERVICE is shown.
INDEX TO STATIONS, pages xviii to xxxvi. and page 1.

WITH A

TRAVELLING MAP OF THE RAILWAYS

SHOWING THE LINES OF NAVIGATION, DISTANCES, &c.

A GENERAL STEAM PACKET DIRECTORY,

ALPHABETICALLY ARRANGED, GIVING THE

DAILY SAILINGS OF ALL THE STEAM VESSELS DURING THE MONTH

TO AND FROM EVERY PORT AND STATION THROUGHOUT THE UNITED KINGDOM;

And the MAIL PACKET ROUTES to all QUARTERS of the GLOBE.

LONDON :—W. J. ADAMS & SONS, 59, FLEET STREET (E.C.).
MANCHESTER :—HENRY BLACKLOCK & Co., EDITORIAL DEPARTMENT, ALBERT SQUARE;
And SHEFFIELD :—14, FARGATE.
LIVERPOOL :—W. H. SMITH & SON, 61, DALE STREET. BIRMINGHAM :—W. H. SMITH & SON, 33, UNION STREET.
BRIGHTON :—H. & C. TREACHER, 1, NORTH STREET. SOUTHAMPTON :—GUTCH & COX, HIGH STREET.
EDINBURGH :—JOHN MENZIES & CO., 12, HANOVER STREET. GLASGOW :—JAMES REID, 144, ARGYLE STREET.
DUBLIN :—CARSON BROTHERS, 7, GRAFTON STREET (Corner of Stephen's Green).
PARIS :—THE GALIGNANI LIBRARY, 224, RUE DE RIVOLI.
BRUSSELS :—M. J. BIL (BRADSHAW'S GUIDE OFFICE), 6 and 7, PASSAGE DES POSTES, BOULEVARD ANSPACH.
AND SOLD BY ALL BOOKSELLERS AND AT ALL RAILWAY STATIONS THROUGHOUT GREAT BRITAIN,
IRELAND, AND THE CONTINENT.

'ENTERED AT STATIONERS' HALL.'

MANSION HOUSE (CITY STATION) FOR WINDSOR, EALING, ACTON, PUTNEY
BRIDGE, HOUNSLOW, OSTERLEY, RICHMOND, KEW GARDENS, HAMMERSMITH, VIA
TEMPLE, CHARING CROSS, WESTMINSTER, VICTORIA, SOUTH KENSINGTON. See back of Map & pages 2 and 180 to 183.

LONDON AND SEASIDE SERVICE, see Back Page of Cover.

ROYAL MAIL ROUTE and SHORTEST SEA PASSAGE between ENGLAND and SCOTLAND and BELFAST and NORTH of IRELAND, via Larne and Stranraer. Sea Passage about 2¼ hours. See page 422

CHAPTER 8

Beyond the Smoke

OUT OF TOWN WITH SHERLOCK

"There are difficulties, Watson. The vocabulary of Bradshaw is nervous and terse, but limited. The selection of words would hardly lend itself to the sending of general messages. We will eliminate Bradshaw."

Sherlock Holmes, *The Valley of Fear*

OPPOSITE: In 1839 George Bradshaw launched the first of his railway guides, so indispensable for Victorians train travelers. Holmes and Watson were among many fictitious characters to consult one: bloodthirsty Count Dracula checked his Bradshaw in preparation for his trip to England.

From the 1830s and the birth of British steam-train travel, the UK rail network burgeoned. By the end of the 19th century, 18,500 miles (29,000km) of track crisscrossed the country, some 150 companies ran trains, and *Bradshaw's Monthly Railway Guide*—the world's first rail-timetables compilation—had grown from eight pages in 1841 to nearly a thousand.

Without the steam train and the guide, Holmes's jaunts beyond the city's purlieus would have been very slow and arduous. So, of course, he had a Bradshaw. *Everybody* had a Bradshaw—at least, everybody who was on the move.

No wonder Watson thought of Bradshaw when it came to decoding a message from Fred Porlock, the weakest link in Moriarty's chain. The key, Holmes had concluded, must be the page number of a *large* book that "anyone may be supposed to possess."

It was a glaring limitation of Bradshaw that, though indispensable to the Victorian gad-about, it was lamentably short on words for the purposes of encryption—when George Bradshaw conceived the work, he simply failed to foresee its being put to such use.

For dashing around town, as we know, Holmes and Watson would for preference use a hansom cab. They did not waste time on tram or omnibus. And it is telling that, though Baker Street Station was on their doorstep, only once do we hear of them taking the Underground—to Aldersgate Street, in *The Red-Headed League*. But, then, the world's first underground railway was not a pleasant ride. When the Circle Line was completed in 1884, *The Times* described it as "a form of mild torture which no person would undergo if he could conveniently help it." In 1890, the City & South London Railway introduced the world's first deep-level line, with trains comprising just three 32-seat carriages. They had no windows to speak of, and the line was soon dubbed "the sardine box railway."

The Tube today is not usually torture outside rush hour, but like our heroes, as we jaunt a little outside the city to some of the more pleasing destinations in Holmes's adventures, we tend to favor the overground train, going underground only when it is expedient. And—because we don't merely see but *observe*—we'll notice the grandeur of the first station on our itinerary.

THE FRENCH CONNECTION

When he was not giving Scotland Yarders lessons in the art of detection, Sherlock Holmes was in demand abroad. In 1891 he was in France, where he had been engaged by the government "upon a matter of supreme importance," as Watson recalled in *The Final Problem*. Back in London, Holmes and Watson boarded the continental express boat train at Victoria Station, sending their baggage through to Paris, though aborting their journey at Canterbury and instead taking a ferry from Newhaven to Dieppe on what everyone feared was the last fateful adventure.

We see how far rail travel had progressed by the airy way in which Watson recorded that "we made our way over the Gemmi Pass, still deep in snow, and so, by way of Interlaken, to Meiringen." Today it is easier than ever. Lunch in Paris? You can board Eurostar at **St Pancras** and be in the French capital in a little more than two hours. There you might visit the Louvre, birthplace of Emile-Jean-Horace Vernet, whose parents stayed there during the French Revolution—in *The Adventure of the Greek Interpreter*, Holmes claims "Vernet, the French artist" among his ancestors.

Or just stay in St Pancras Station and gaze up at a Victorian work of art, William Henry Barlow's single-span cast-iron train-shed roof, a 243-foot (73m) arch, rising to 100 feet (30.5m) above the tracks. When the station opened in 1868 this was the tallest and widest station roof ever built, creating the largest enclosed space in the world.

Sixty million bricks went into the building of George Gilbert Scott's 300-room Gothic Revival hotel, the Midland Grand, which formed part of the station and its frontage. Having opened in the

1870s, it ceased operations as a hotel in 1935 and became railway offices. In the philistine 1960s it was threatened with demolition, and it stood empty from the late 1980s until the mid-1990s, when restoration began. Today, at the renamed **St Pancras Renaissance London**, you can raise a glass at Europe's longest champagne bar. But here's a sobering thought—no champagne toasts were drunk at the Midland Grand at the wedding breakfast of Hosmer Angel and the cruelly deceived Mary Sutherland, who was left standing at the altar in *A Case of Identity*.

BELOW: Great Scott! The entrance hall to George Gilbert Scott's Gothic Revival Midland Grand hotel at St Pancras Station soon after its opening. It was equipped with such state-of-the-art amenities as speaking tubes and "ascending chambers" (elevators).

SCHOOL ON THE HILL

Handy though it would have been, there was no **Marylebone Station** when Holmes and Watson conveyed Helen Stoner on the morning train to **Harrow** and into the care of her maiden aunt, Miss Honoria Westphail, after her stepfather, Dr Grimesby Roylott, was fatally bitten by his own venomous snake in *The Adventure of the Speckled Band*. The Marylebone terminus of the last main line into London did not open until March 1899. The redbrick station building was designed by the engineer HW Braddock, and in the 20th century was compared—by the Poet Laureate John Betjeman, no less—to a branch public library. But trains serve the Chilterns, and you can be in Harrow on the Hill in just 12 minutes from here.

Don't be discouraged by Steve Dixie's warning to Holmes that his life would be in danger "out Harrow way" in *The Adventure of the Three Gables* (a story with which few Holmes fans feel comfortable). In 1899, Grove Hill in Harrow on the Hill was the site of the first recorded car crash in Britain in which the driver was killed, and a commemorative plaque cautions "TAKE HEED," but Harrow on the Hill retains a ye-olde-tea-shoppe village feel with no lurking air of menace.

The eponymous hill is crowned by the Church of St Mary's, founded in the 11th century by Archbishop Lanfranc. A plaque by the door commemorates Allegra, Lord Byron's illegitimate daughter who died at the age of five. The "mad, bad and dangerous" poet attended Harrow School, founded in the reign of Elizabeth I. There he met John FitzGibbon, 2nd Earl of Clare, and George John Sackville-West, 5th Earl De La Warr, and the three students became enduring friends. "My school friendships were with me passions (for I was always violent)," Byron afterward wrote.

Harrow School buildings include the Vaughan Library by George Gilbert Scott of Midland Grand fame (page 134) and the Victorian chapel. You can visit the Harrow's Old Speech Room Gallery, built in 1819–21, and admire collections

ABOVE: Harrow students in uniform tailcoats and straw boaters. Old Harrovian (Sherlock) Cumberbatch, aged 13, impressed his drama teacher with his "intuition and intellect" as he auditioned for the part of a French maid in a farce, making play with a feather duster.

that include Greek and Egyptian antiquities and busts of old Harrovians.

Alumni include Sir Winston Churchill, the playwright Terence Rattigan (who made his stage debut as Titania, Queen of the Fairies, in a school production of *A Midsummer Night's Dream*), and Benedict Cumberbatch, who was an arts scholar and—as if you need to be told!—went on to star in *Sherlock*.

HAMPSTEAD HIGHS

It's the dead of night in Hampstead, and a fire blazes in the grate of the study at Appledore Towers. Milverton, "the king of blackmailers" in *The Adventure of Charles Augustus Milverton*, lies dead on the floor, shot by a female victim of his extortion. Holmes and Watson, behind the curtain, have witnessed the whole thing, before feeding the flames with the letters that would compromise Lady Eva Blackwell, and scaling the back wall to escape from their pursuers "across the huge expanse of Hampstead Heath."

RIGHT: Pond life. The city's largest open parkland, Hampstead Heath, is famous for its ponds. A music hall song celebrated 'Appy 'Ampstead, which was a popular destination for London day-trippers—but for Holmes and Watson it proved hostile territory.

The two came here, as was their custom, by hansom, alighting at Church Row and walking for a quarter of an hour to Milverton's mansion. We might instead board a Northern Line Tube train to Hampstead Station, head up Holly Hill and take a right on Holly Bush Hill, leading to Hampstead Grove. Here we find **Fenton House**, a 17th-century merchant's residence, a National Trust property, and the oldest surviving mansion in a part of London which is replete with great houses. One cannot say for sure that this was the model for Appledore Towers, but it does have a walled garden, and the visitor enters through an impressive gate, as our furtive duo did.

The house is filled with porcelain and antique keyboard instruments. From the balcony you can look across London, to see the dome of St Paul's amid a forest of cranes.

A great, airy upland at one of the highest points in London, **Hampstead Heath** is a mix of ancient woodlands and grasslands rich in wildlife. Of numerous ponds, three are designated for bathing—one for men, one for women, the third for both sexes—fed by the headwater springs of the River Fleet.

Skirting the heath, as Holmes and Watson did, head north from the station onto Spaniards Road. After just over half a mile (1km) you come to the Spaniards Inn, one of London's oldest pubs, where **John Keats**, they claim, wrote *Ode to a Nightingale*. The poet's former home, now the Keats House museum and literary center, is reached by going left out of the station and down the hill, then left on Downshire Hill and right on Keats Grove to No. 10. Holmes would not have cared a fig about it, if as Watson surmised his interest in literature was nil—but we doubt it.

OF BARONS AND MONARCHY

In *The Adventure of the Illustrious Client*, Holmes took a hansom cab to call on Baron Adelbert Gruner, aristocrat of crime, at Vernon Lodge, near **Kingston upon Thames**. The town is 12 miles (19km) from Charing Cross—a pleasant run out for the cab horse accustomed to slogging 40 miles (64km) a day around the city. And, for the cabbie, a fare of sixpence a mile (1.6km), with a gratuity on top—nice work, if you could get it!

For us it is less than half an hour by train from **Waterloo** (where Holmes had supper upon arriving from Aldershot in *The Adventure of the Crooked Man*). The then busiest train station in Great Britain was, in the late 1890s, holy chaos, with 50,000 passengers alighting there every day. In *Three Men in a Boat* (1889), his humorous account of a boating holiday on the Thames, Doyle's friend Jerome K Jerome sends up the experience of trying to find out from which platform the Kingston train would depart: "… nobody at Waterloo ever does know where a train is going to start from, or where a train when it does start is going to, or anything about it…" We should have no such problems.

Holmes's "near Kingston" is not much help in the matter of the whereabouts of Vernon Lodge, but we follow the money up Kingston Hill toward the Coombe Estate, "millionaires' row", and turn down Warren Road. It's quite a walk, but is only a quarter of an hour or so by bus (K3 or 85) from Cromwell Road Bus Station in the town center.

Watson, for his part, did give us clues. A "beautiful house and grounds… A long winding drive with banks of rare shrubs… built by a South African gold king in the days of the great boom… imposing in its size and solidity." And if we cannot give you Vernon Lodge—we can give you a fine substitute—**Warren House** is indeed a beautiful mansion, solid, imposing. And though Watson says nothing of mullioned windows, of the three gables, the diaper brickwork, or the stone outer porch with crest above—recalling, instead, corner turrets—it could even be the real thing, disguised.

The house was built in 1860 on land leased from the Duke of Cambridge, for Hugh Hammersley of Cox & Co, bankers to the British Army. The very bank, indeed, in whose vaults Watson kept his battered tin dispatch box, crammed with papers relating to the cases tackled by Holmes. Hammersley acquired part of the neighboring Coombe Wood Nursery, famous for its specimen rhododendrons and magnolias brought from the Far East.

In 1884 the house was sold to George Grenfell Glyn, 2nd Baron Wolverton, and extended by the architect George Devey. In 1895 the lease was sold on to George Cawston, stockbroker and city financier, an early director of Cecil Rhodes's British South Africa Company, and in 1907 Lady Mary (Minnie) Paget bought the freehold. Although set in 1902, *The Adventure of the Illustrious Client* was not written until 1924, 17 years after she purchased it. Like Doyle, Minnie's husband, General Sir Arthur Henry Fitzroy Paget, served in South Africa in the Second Boer War. In a lesser way than Doyle, Paget was a novelist, writing as Mr Fitzroy. Minnie was known for her beauty, her fabulous collection of jewelry, and her literary salons—her home was frequented by the "leading lights of literature and art."

Warren House, Vernon Lodge? Vernon Lodge, Warren House? Winding drive? Check. Shrubs? Check. Baron in residence? Check. A South African connection? Check!

None of this is to say that Arthur Conan Doyle knew the place and used it as his model for

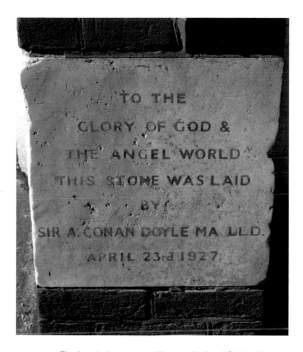

ABOVE: The foundation stone at Kingston National Spiritualist Church, laid by Arthur Conan Doyle three years before his death. To the end, he professed a belief in the afterlife, despite having created the rational, un-superstitious super-sleuth.

Christopher Wren for William and Mary, it more recently provided locations for Guy Ritchie's *A Game of Shadows*. Not only did we get to see the Tudor kitchens, but the Privy Garden stood in for a Parisian park, while the Inner Courtyard served as Moriarty's college entrance.

GREENWICH FOR STARGAZERS

In *The Sign of Four* the police pursued *The Aurora* downriver past Greenwich, which was served by London's first passenger railroad —the London and Greenwich Railway. One of the world's oldest railway viaducts and the first elevated railway line, it opened in 1836. An unbroken line of 878 arches forms a viaduct that carries trains the 3½ miles (5.5km) from London Bridge Station—a triumph of the ingenuity of retired Royal Engineers officer Colonel GT Landemann.

Alternatively, you can take a train from Cannon Street, or the driverless Docklands Light Railway (DLR), alighting at Cutty Sark for Maritime Greenwich. You might even come by river, from the pier at Embankment, Tower, or

Gruner's abode. It is a capital mistake, as every Holmes scholar is aware, to theorize before one has the data—to twist facts to suit theories, not theories to suit facts. So all we can say for sure is that Warren House, now a hotel, does a slap-up afternoon tea. Booking is essential.

Kingston's defining advantage is its riverside location—though some come to attend the National Spiritualist Church, its foundation stone laid by Sir Arthur Conan Doyle in 1927. A stroll toward Surbiton along the Queen's Promenade is recommended (boats, ducks, swans) but, better still, you can cross the river and walk through Home Park or (from March to October) take a boat to Hampton Court Palace.

Built by Cardinal Wolsey, Hampton Court Palace was gifted to Henry VIII at that great king's "suggestion." Much made over by Sir

BELOW: Ticket to ride. The London and Greenwich Railway was the brainchild of a bullish retired Royal Engineers colonel who conceived a viaduct to carry commuter trains—a thing of beauty that bestrode the landscape, now subsumed by urban sprawl.

ABOVE: Sunrise over the Old Royal Naval College, designed by Sir Christopher Wren for Mary II as the "darling object" of her life, a charitable hospital for sailors. The two halves frame the Queen's House and Greenwich Park. It served as a filming location in *A Game of Shadows*.

Westminster, alighting at Greenwich Pier, near the heroic little tea clipper the *Cutty Sark* (launched in 1869) and the Old Royal Naval College. There is also an option to cross from the Isle of Dogs via the Greenwich Foot Tunnel, designed by Alexander Binnie and opened in 1902. The echoing, white-tiled tunnel, which has an internal diameter of 9 feet (2.7m), is 1,215 feet (370m) long and 50 feet (15m) deep. Check for closures before you go.

The building now known as the **Old Royal Naval College** was commissioned in 1694 by Queen Mary II as the Royal Hospital for Seamen, a home for elderly, wounded, or ill sailors. Only one thing, she told her architect, Sir Christopher Wren—it must not spoil her view from the

Queen's House. (The queen in question, Anne of Denmark, wife of James I, did not live to see the completion of the building designed for her by Inigo Jones.) Wren's solution was to build his Baroque masterpiece in two parts. Although it took over half a century to complete, from 1696 till 1751, the seamen were admitted from 1706. Wren worked with Nicholas Hawksmoor and then was succeeded by John Vanbrugh, working to Wren's designs. Viewed from across the river, the college buildings and the Queen's House form a single symmetrical sweep. The view from Greenwich, of the massed towers of Canary Wharf on the north bank, is less sublime.

So spectacular was James Thornhill's Painted Hall—intended for a dining room—that the old seadogs were not allowed inside it. The hospital became the Royal Naval College in 1869. It now houses the University of Greenwich in fine style and makes frequent movie appearances, not least in Guy Ritchie's *A Game of Shadows.* A street scene was filmed in Queen Anne's Court for the 2009 *Sherlock Holmes.* Tours are available.

Walk down Park Row to find the riverside **Trafalgar Tavern**, much as it was in Holmes's day. Grade I listed, it was so beloved of Charles Dickens that he used it in *Our Mutual Friend* for the wedding feast of Bella Wilfer and John Harman.

The pub was famous for its whitebait suppers— small fry straight from the Thames. Whitebait is still on the menu, but not, fortunately, fished from these waters! The building dates from 1837 and was designed by Joseph Kay. A statue of Horatio Nelson gazes from the cobbled terrace, the naval treaty in his right hand.

The advent of the railways had an impact on public attitudes to timekeeping. Imagine George Bradshaw's nightmare when he first started to compile his timetables, with different parts of the country observing local time—the east side

BELOW: Built in Queen Victoria's coronation year, the Trafalgar Tavern is lapped by the Thames. Drinkers could have watched from the bow windows or the pub terrace as the police pursued *The Aurora* in *The Sign of Four.*

of the country being half an hour ahead of the west. All at once, punctuality was everything, and the pressure was on to adopt standard time.

In 1884, at a conference in Washington DC, Greenwich was chosen as the site of the Prime Meridian of the world. Walk up the steep slope of Greenwich Park to the **Royal Observatory,** and you can straddle the line of longitude, placing your feet in the east and west hemispheres. The Royal Observatory, which is now a museum, was commissioned from Christopher Wren by Charles II in 1675. The building's name, Flamsteed House, recalls John Flamsteed, Astronomer Royal. Flamsteed was appointed by Charles II to "apply himself with the most exact care and diligence to the rectifying of the tables of the motions of the heavens, and the places of the fixed stars, in order to the finding out of longitude for perfecting navigation and astronomy."

Holmes professed ignorance of Copernican theory in *A Study in Scarlet* and avowed indifference to whether the sun revolved around the earth or vice versa. This, however, was belied in *The Adventure of the Greek Interpreter* by his discussion of the causes of the change in the obliquity of the ecliptic, and by his casual reference in *The Adventure of the Musgrave Ritual* to "the personal equation, as the astronomers have dubbed it." But, then, Holmes was constantly developing and refining his skills. To that end he might well have visited the Observatory—his interest piqued by the knowledge that Professor Moriarty was the celebrated author of *The Dynamics of an Asteroid*, "a book which," Holmes told Watson in *The Valley of Fear*, "ascends to such rarefied heights of pure mathematics that it is said that there was no man in the scientific press capable of criticizing it." He would have liked today's Planetarium!

Synchronize watches and aim to be outside the Observatory for 12.55pm, when the red time ball on the top—one of the world's first public time signals—begins its upward journey, to come plummeting down on the dot of 1pm, as it has done since 1833.

If you exit the park gates and cross the main road, you find yourself in **Blackheath**, where John Hector McFarlane lived in *The Adventure of the Norwood Builder*, and where a young Watson had played rugby for the local club. He took a train from here to London Bridge (as you can, too) in *The Adventure of the Retired Colorman*.

Arthur Conan Doyle had a special attachment to Blackheath, for here, in 1897, he met and fell in love with Jean Leckie, a vivacious mezzo-soprano 14 years his junior who was living with her parents while training to be a singer. Touie was by this time very sick. She had been diagnosed with "galloping consumption" in October 1893, but defied a dire prognosis and survived until 1906. A year later, Doyle married Jean. In the intervening years they had conducted what the author always insisted was a "platonic" affair, although "unconsummated" might be more precise.

In the Georgian era many wealthy Londoners forsook the grimy city for the healthy uplands of Greenwich and Blackheath, hence the great many fine period homes that are found there. The Blackheath Paragon does not describe Jean Leckie but a crescent of 14 Georgian houses dating from 1793–1807 and designed by Michael Searles— seven pairs of semi-detached houses, linked by colonnades, at one corner of the heath. No tenant was to practice "art, mystery or trade"; the likes of schoolteachers and fishmongers were also excluded, although this did not prevent Misses Eliza Robertson and Charlotte Sharp—who ran a school in Greenwich and were accused of fraud and cross-dressing—from moving in.

Blackheath was for many centuries a place of historic welcome and pageantry for visitors to these shores from across the Channel. In January 1540, Anne of Cleves, whom Henry VIII just couldn't fancy, was greeted by the king and London's lord mayor, aldermen, and citizenry in a grand ceremony on the heath, from where she was escorted to the royal palace at Greenwich to become Henry's fourth wife. There can, though, have been no more memorable day than May 29,

ABOVE: The elegant Georgian crescent of The Paragon on the heath, the houses linked by colonnades. Blackheath was the home of Jean Leckie, Doyle's second-wife-in-waiting. It has seen many historic comings and goings, being on the route from the Channel Ports.

1660, when Charles II was feted here amid scenes of jubilation, upon his return from exile. No Charles II, no Royal Observatory.

Jude Law, who played Dr Watson in the 2009 *Sherlock Holmes* movie, grew up in Blackheath, where he attended John Ball Primary School. It was named for the Lollard priest John Ball, who preached to the participants at their rallying point on the heath for Wat Tyler's Peasants' Revolt of 1381. Having exhorted them to "cast off the yoke of bondage, and recover liberty," Ball was executed later that year in the presence of Richard II.

Blackheath village is always busy on high days and holidays, but it *is* indisputably a village, with independent shops and cafes on the delightfully named Tranquil Vale. There is even a violin workshop if your Strad needs restoring.

NORWOOD—HIGH AND LOW

There are, in southeast London, three Norwoods—South, Upper, and West—each with its own station (Norwood Junction, Crystal Palace, West Norwood), with train services from London Bridge and Victoria—but no Underground station. Arthur Conan Doyle lived from 1891 to 1894 at 12 Tennison Road, South Norwood, and played for the local cricket team. In *The Sign of Four*, Athelney Jones was at South Norwood Police Station.

However, we start at **Upper Norwood,** also commonly known as Crystal Palace. The area enjoyed a Victorian heyday after the Great Exhibition of 1851 in Hyde Park, when Joseph Paxton's wondrous glasshouse was dismantled and re-erected at the top on Penge Common, by

143

Sydenham Hill, between 1852 and 1854. There are still those who can remember how the night sky blazed crimson in November 1936, when "the people's palace" burned down. And, despite destruction of another kind in the 1960s, some 19th-century gems—one, at least, an absolute treasure—survive on Church Road, Upper Norwood, and its tributaries, to help us picture Pondicherry Lodge, where Major John Sholto retired to live in luxury after prospering in India in *The Sign of Four.*

There is something romantic in the remnants of stone balustrading, arches, and terraces in **Crystal Palace Park**—here a sphinx, there a headless statue. The Palace was still standing, of course, when Grant Munro, uneasy in his mind, walked for an hour or so in the grounds, in *The Adventure of the Yellow Face.* An ornately tiled subway, once lit by chandeliers and leading beneath the road to the long-since demolished

High Level Station, may yet be opened to the public. The Victorian Tea Maze has been replanted. But the unique attractions of this park of woods, ponds, and grassland are its concrete "dinosaurs," built by Benjamin Waterhouse Hawkins, in 1853—only a decade after the Hunterian Museum's curator Richard Owen coined the name "dinosaur." There are more than 30 of these life-size sculptures, Grade I listed monuments, the first of their kind ever in the world, reflecting the state of knowledge of the day.

Before we leave Upper Norwood, a word about one stellar canine detective. When the Jules Rimet Trophy was stolen from a display cabinet in the run-up to the 1966 FIFA World Cup, a dog named Pickles—surely the equal of the bird-stuffer's hound Toby in *The Adventure of the Missing Three-Quarter*—took it upon himself to do a bit of nose work and ran the silverware to ground under a hedge on Beulah Hill.

ABOVE: The Crystal Palace "dinosaurs" are more than 30 "life-size" sculptures representing 15 genera of extinct creatures. They range across a wide sweep of prehistory, with wildly varying degrees of accuracy and Victorian verve.

West Norwood, formerly called "Lower Norwood," was home to the reclusive bachelor Jonas Oldacre, the builder of *The Adventure of the Norwood Builder* fame. There is no hope of locating Deep Dene House "at the Sydenham End of the road of that name" (this slightly defies mapping), and, with no disrespect to the living, the area's glory is its cemetery. Located on Norwood Road, it is the second of the "Magnificent Seven" burial parks (see Brompton Cemetery, page 105). It was built in the Gothic Revival style in 1836–7 and is reckoned to have London's finest collection of sepulchral monuments. The aficionado of funerary art will have a field day. And there is a Holmes connection—of sorts. Here, in a simple grave lies Isabella Beeton (who died in childbirth, aged 28, having gained fame for her books on cookery and household management). A stone commemorates Mrs Beeton and her husband,

Samuel Orchart Beeton, who in November 1887 published *A Study in Scarlet* in *Beeton's Christmas Annual*, and introduced the world to Sherlock Holmes.

Walking north from West Norwood, cutting across Brockwell Park, with its lido, would bring you to ever more trendy Brixton, home to Stanley Hopkins in *The Adventure of Black Peter* and the Tangeys in *The Adventure of the Naval Treaty*. There, Nathan Garrideb was last heard of, in a nursing home, never to recover from the shock of dissipated dreams in *The Adventure of the Three Garridebs*. When Sherlock Holmes came by here, the land was partly rural. In *The Adventure of the Blue Carbuncle* Mrs Oakshott of 117 Brixton Road was a supplier of eggs and poultry—so don't be entirely surprised to find, on Blenheim Gardens, off Brixton Hill, within sight of Brixton Prison, right here in the inner city, an early 19th-century windmill.

AFTERWORD

The Immortal Sherlock Holmes

"I trust that age doth not wither nor custom stale my infinite variety"

Sherlock Holmes, *The Empty House*

OPPOSITE: Narrow scrapes and great escapes. Holmes and Watson in the
BBC's emotional rollercoaster first series of *Sherlock*.

As no reader needs reminding, in *The Final Problem*, published in December 1893, Arthur Conan Doyle dispatched our hero in a fight to the death with his nemesis, Professor Moriarty, at the Reichenbach Falls. It was an act of "refined, cold-blooded, deliberate murder" by the author, worthy of Jack Stapleton (real name Rodger Baskerville). "Killed Holmes," Doyle jotted in his notebook, with chilling nonchalance. He would later plead self-defense: "If I had not killed Sherlock Holmes, I verily believe he would have killed me."

Loyal readers were distraught. At the offices of *The Strand Magazine*, which had published the story, letters poured in by the sack-load, some pleading for resurrection, some threatening the editor and author. "You brute!" wrote one woman to Doyle. Some 20,000 readers cancelled their subscriptions.

The writer was unrepentant, but then what would you expect from a man who had ignored the entreaties of his own dear mother to spare the life of his detective? He was, he said, sick of Holmes. He had higher literary ambitions. It was never meant to go this far.

It is easy for us today; we can read the entire canon at will. And we can only imagine how it felt in the nine Holmes-less wilderness years, when it seemed that Sherlock had been wiped from the face of the earth.

Finally, in 1899, there were stirrings of life, when the American actor–playwright William Gillette brought Holmes to the stage. Doyle saw that there was a fortune in the project, but seemed so much to have washed his hands of his creature that, we recall, when Gillette asked if the script could see Sherlock Holmes married—unthinkable, surely?—Doyle responded, "You may marry him, murder him, or do what you like to him." Even so, he permitted himself a moment of compunction. On reading Gillette's adaptation he murmured, "It's good to see the old chap back."

Gillette's play, *Sherlock Holmes: a Drama in Four Acts*, made its stage debut in Buffalo, New York, in October 1899, and went on to take Broadway by

ABOVE: Fall guys. Holmes (Jeremy Brett in the Granada TV series) and Moriarty had plunged to certain death over the Reichenbach Falls, as it seemed to Watson.

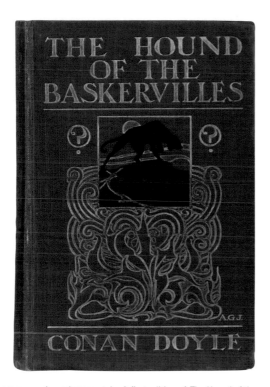

ABOVE: A posthumous tale. A first edition of *The Hound of the Baskervilles*. Fans seized upon it thankfully, but the narrative was told in retrospect, with their hero still officially dead. They had to wait another year for Doyle to resurrect him.

storm, although attracting mixed reviews in London (page 91). Over a 30-year period Gillette would reprise the title role some 1,300 times.

Two years after the stage premiere, Doyle did not so much repent as relent, bowing to public pressure to breathe life anew into Sherlock. His most famous novel, *The Hound of the Baskervilles*, was first serialized in 1901 (and published as a novel in 1902), but it was told retrospectively; Holmes was still officially missing, presumed dead—indeed, "dead and damned," as his creator would have it.

In 1903, all that changed with publication of *The Adventure of the Empty House*, set in 1894, and—let joy be unconfined!—with Holmes once more alive and well and living on Baker Street. Subscriptions to *The Strand Magazine* enjoyed a 30,000 bounce.

Back in 1886, when he sat down to write *A Study in Scarlet*, bringing into being the world's first consulting detective, the young author had not the faintest notion that he was conjuring the most enduring fictional character in literary history, and the most frequently portrayed. To date Holmes has incarnated in more than 300 movies, as well as countless radio, television, and stage productions. There have been puppet shows, comic strips, animated cartoons. Recent times have brought us the hugely successful BBC *Sherlock*, Guy Ritchie's movies, CBS's *Elementary*, Ian McKellen as the elderly Sherlock, based on Mitch Cullin's novel *A Slight Trick of the Mind*. What next, we only wait to see. Almost 140 years after that seminal novel, Holmes's appeal is stronger than ever. And, no, custom has not staled his infinite variety.

AGELESS, INVINCIBLE

The first serious attempt to bring Sherlock Holmes to the cinema was in 1905 with a silent-film version of Doyle's 1890 novel *The Sign of Four* entitled *The Adventures of Sherlock Holmes*. There followed, in a decade, more than fifty silent movies, mainly Danish-, German-, or French-made, or Anglo–French collaborations.

In 1914, *Der Hund von Baskervilles* came to German screens, the tale very loosely based on the original novel. In England, meanwhile, *A Study in Scarlet*, starring a studio hand named James Bragington (chosen for his perceived likeness to Holmes), became the first British feature-length Sherlock Holmes movie. Two years later, the actor Harry Arthur Saintsbury, who had previously played Holmes onstage, replaced Bragington to star in *The Valley of Fear*.

Also that year, William Gillette, now in his sixties, appeared as Holmes in *Sherlock Holmes* on the silent screen, and although consensus at the time held that he was too old for the role, when a negative of that movie, long supposed lost, came to light in 2014, it was as if the Great Agra Treasure had been found at the back of a filing cabinet.

Another older actor, Eille Norwood, was 59 when he stepped into Holmes's dressing gown and Persian slippers to star in a series of movies for the Stoll Film Company, shot at the newly built Cricklewood Studios in north London, from 1921. A man with a rich sense of humor, Norwood reveled in the disguises he had to assume, on occasion even fooling fellow cast members and crew. In a three-year period, Norwood (real name Anthony Edward Brett) played Holmes 47 times, in 45 short films and two feature-length films—more than any other actor. For Doyle, Norwood's command of the character was "masterful."

The first Sherlock Holmes sound movie was released in 1929, a year before Doyle's death. Paramount's *The Return of Sherlock Holmes*, starred Clive Brook, whose matinee idol looks would strike us today as really not the thing.

Among the most memorable of later Holmes actors, one thinks of Basil Rathbone, who starred in no fewer than 14 Sherlock Holmes movies between 1939 and 1946, with Nigel Bruce as Dr Watson. Only the first two of the series, made by 20th Century Fox, were set in the Victorian era, the rest being updated to the 1940s. The film studios Universal rationalized this by saying, "The character of Sherlock Holmes, created by Sir Arthur Conan Doyle, is ageless, invincible, and unchanging. In solving significant problems of the present day, he remains, as ever, the supreme master of deductive reasoning."

In 1964 it was Douglas Wilmer's turn to don the deerstalker, as the first television Sherlock in the BBC's production of *The Speckled Band*. In the following year he starred in a further 12 stories.

Many fans have vivid memories of Jeremy Brett, who starred in the 41 episodes of the Granada TV series *The Adventures of Sherlock Holmes* in the decade from 1984. Brett strove to be the greatest Sherlock Holmes ever, the very embodiment of the man, until he confessed, "Holmes has become the dark side of the moon for me… It has all got too dangerous."

Brett was to top a 2014 poll as the Greatest Sherlock Holmes—ahead even of Benedict Cumberbatch and Robert Downey Jr, but give these relative newcomers time.

HOLMES IS WHERE THE HEART IS

"They say," wrote Doyle in his autobiography, "a man is never properly appreciated until he is dead, and the general protest against my summary

OPPOSITE: The suave English-born actor Clive Brook in Paramount's 1929 *The Return of Sherlock Holmes*—the first sound movie to feature the great detective—with H Reeves-Smith as Watson. Like Holmes, Brook was an accomplished violinist.

RIGHT: Jeremy Brett smokes the calabash-style pipe we associate with Sherlock. He starred in 41 episodes of the Granada TV series from 1984 to 1994, and confessed he found the role harder to play than Macbeth or Hamlet, because Doyle said Holmes was a man without a heart—all brain.

execution of Holmes taught me how many and numerous were his friends." Many and numerous back then—innumerable now.

All the world loves Sherlock Holmes. His adventures have been translated into almost every language and the stories have never been out of print. The Egyptian Khedive and the last true Ottoman potentate were not the only fans in high places. In the USSR Holmes was commended to the Red Army as the epitome of "magnificent strength and great culture."

The Holmes canon has generated a vast slew of secondary literature, me-too novels, spoofs, spin-offs, prequels, sequels, scholarly essays and dissertations, encyclopedias, annotated collections, author biographies—and, well, guidebooks to Holmes's London.

There are literally hundreds of fan clubs and appreciation societies—not just the London Sherlockians, but the Baker Street Irregulars of

New York (founded 1934) and such scions as the Dancing Men of Providence, the Speckled Band of Boston, the Six Napoleons of Baltimore… Hail to the Delaware Deerstalkers, the Creeping Men of Cleveland, the Dying Detectives of Minneapolis, the Friends of Baron Gruner, the Saxe-Coburg Squares, the Baskerville Hall Club of Sweden, Le Cercle Littéraire de l'Escarbouche Bleue, the Copenhagen Speckled Gang, the Bruce-Partington Planners, Gli Amici de Sherlock Holmes, the Dead-Headed League, the Silver Blazers, the Agra Treasurers, the Reichenbach Falls Lemmings, the Napoleons of Crime…

The BBC's *Sherlock* has millions of devoted fans in China, where Holmes is known as "Curly Fu" (a reference to Benedict Cumberbatch's hair) and Watson is "Peanut" (which originates from the Chinese translation of Martin Freeman's name, "Hua Sheng" sounding like the Mandarin word for nut).

ABOVE: Benedict Cumberbatch and Martin Freeman as Holmes and Watson have brought the great consulting detective and his sidekick into the 21st century and won over a new generation of fans.

There is a Sherlock-themed café in Shanghai, as well as a Sherlock Holmes Pub at the Ramses Hilton, and one in Stockholm. In Japan, Sherlock has long been popular—an abridged version of *The Man with the Twisted Lip* was published way back in 1894, followed in 1899 by a newspaper series adaptation of *A Study in Scarlet*. The Japan Sherlock Holmes Club, founded in 1977, erected a statue to him 11 years later, in Karuizawa Town, and today has some 900 members.

At the Reichenbach Falls in Germany a memorial plate at the funicular station commemorates the terrible events of *The Final Problem*.

In the English Church at nearby Meiringen in Switzerland a Sherlock Holmes Museum was opened in 1991 under the auspices of the Sherlock Holmes Society of London. It includes another faithful reimagining of the cozy Baker Street sitting room (deerstalkers and magnifying glasses are on sale in the souvenir shop).

There is something deeply heartwarming about the willingness—indeed, the eagerness—of men and women around the world to form societies, to dress up in Victorian garb, to travel to meet their foreign counterparts, to celebrate and endlessly to share their insights and researches into a man who existed first in the mind of an ebullient author who came to loathe him, and for ever after in the world's collective imagination.

Not only can age not wither Sherlock Holmes, but custom only adds more and more to his infinite variety, to the great gaiety of nations.

The "real" Sherlock Holmes

In a backhanded way, in *A Study in Scarlet*, Doyle acknowledged a debt to an earlier author and his *Murders in the Rue Morgue*. "You remind me of Edgar Allen Poe's Dupin," Watson told Holmes. "I had no idea that such individuals existed outside of stories." "No doubt," responded Holmes, "you think that you are complimenting me… Now, in my opinion, Dupin was a very inferior fellow. That trick of his of breaking in on his friends' thoughts with an apropos remark after a quarter of an hour's silence is really very showy and superficial."

This was Doyle being playful. Absolutely there was something of Dupin in Sherlock Holmes, as he confided to Robert Louis Stevenson, but it is widely known that the chief inspiration for the character was Dr Joseph Bell, a professor at the University of Edinburgh Medical School in Doyle's student days. One of the fathers of forensic pathology, Bell "singled out" Doyle to be his outpatients clerk.

The older man had a talent not only for diagnosing disease but also for divining his patients' backgrounds, occupations, and characters from what he gleaned from appearances. In one instance he announced that the fellow before him had not long been discharged from the army, and had served as a non-commissioned officer with a Highland regiment stationed in Barbados. "You see, gentleman," Bell explained, "the man was a respectful man but did not remove his hat. They do not in the army, but he would have learned civilian ways had he been long discharged. He has an air of authority and he is obviously Scottish. As to Barbados, his complaint is elephantiasis, which is West Indian and not British."

Elementary!

"Sherlock Holmes," wrote Doyle, "is the literary embodiment… of my memory of a professor of medicine at Edinburgh University." To Bell himself he wrote, "It is most certainly to you I owe Sherlock Holmes."

Bell's response? "You are yourself Sherlock Holmes and well you know it."

ABOVE: Professor Joseph Bell, of whom Doyle professed that Holmes was "The living embodiment… He would sit in the patients' waiting-room with a face like a Red Indian and diagnose the people as they came in, before they had even opened their mouths."

FURTHER READING

The Man Who Created Sherlock Holmes—The life and times of Sir Arthur Conan Doyle,
Andrew Lycett, Free Press.

Arthur Conan Doyle— A life in letters, Jon Lellenberg, Daniel Stashower, Charles Foley (editors),
Harper Perennial.

Toilers in London; or Inquiries Concerning Female Labor in the Metropolis, anon, 1889,
through The Dictionary of Victorian London.

London Fogs, Hon. R Russell, Dodo Press.

London, a Pilgrimage, Blanchard Jerrold with Gustave Doré (illustrator), Anthem Press.

The Horse-World of Victorian London, WJ Gordon, Long Riders' Guild Press (also online).

***The Great Stink of London: Sir Joseph Bazalgette and the Cleansing of the Victorian
Metropolis***, Stephen Halliday, The History Press.

A Visit to Newgate, Charles Dickens, "Sketches by Boz", online.

William Gillette: America's Sherlock Holmes, Henry Zecher, Xlibris

Edward Linley Sambourne's diaries, online via the Royal Borough of Kensington and Chelsea (RBKC)
website.

A Victorian Household: Based on the Diaries of Marion Sambourne, Shirley Nicholson, Sutton
Illustrated History Paperbacks.

The Wanderings of a Spiritualist, Sir Arthur Conan Doyle, online.

The Charles Booth online archive, http://booth.lse.ac.uk/

Dr Joseph Bell: The Original Sherlock Holmes, Robert Hume, Stone Publishing House.

PRINTER'S DEVILRY

Did you spot all the references to stories and characters lurking in the text?

Page 20: **Silver Blaze** was just "Blaze." Page 32: The **King of Bohemia** may or may not have bought his cloaks at Henry Poole. Page 39: the **carbuncle** was not to be **blue**. Page 41: in view of health and safety concerns, it is not recommended that you clamber up on **the lion's mane**. Page 43: Charles Peace's violin is among his possessions, but not **his last bow**. Page 44: "**The crooked man**" does not do justice to the gentleman Raffles. Page 47**: A case of identity**—indeed. Page 48: **The man with the twisted lip**— Charles Peace did not just **twist his lip**, but his entire face. Page 52: you will seek in vain for **the Great Agra Treasure**. Page 57: there is no **engineer's thumb** and no **devil's foot** in the collection. Page 70: Nelson took on not **six Napoleons**—just Bonaparte. Time will tell if there is a **beryl coronet** or **gold pince-nez** in the capsule. The **Speckled Band** has not played in Embankment Gardens. Page 82: the "**red circle**" should read "**Cologne Circle**." Page 84: **Wisteria** is no part of Freemasonry. Page 95: **copper beeches** and **a yellow face** of the sun are not guaranteed. Page 99**: Harding brothers** do not trade here. Page 101: "**Giant rat of Sumatra**" should read "giant sloth of the Americas." Page 104: **The empty house**— empty, at least, of residents. Page 105: Benjamin Baud did not follow **the Bruce-Partington plans**; "**Charles Augustus Milverton**" should read "Henry Augustus Mears." Page 109: no **five orange pips**, no **Black Peter, cardboard box** trick or **Lady Frances Carfax**. Page 116: **Jabez Wilson** is a red herring. Page 118 and 119: **the Greek interpreter** and **the stockbroker's clerk** are teases. Page 121: "**Mazarin Stone**" should read "Sorcerer's Stone" (US) or "Philosopher's Stone" (UK). Page 122: there is no **Straubenzee's workshop**. Page 134: "**the three students**" should read "three schoolboys." Page 138: Warren House has more than **three gables**. Page 141: no **naval treaty**—and no right hand.

LIST OF PLACES

18 Stafford Terrace
W8 7BH
rbkc.gov.uk/subsites/
museums/18staffordterrace1.
aspx

221B Baker Street
NW1 6XE
sherlock-holmes.co.uk

Admiralty
WC2N 5DS

Bank of England
ECR2 8AH
bankofengland.co.uk

Berkeley Square
W1J 5AX

Berry Bros & Rudd
SW1A 1EG
bbr.com

Bow Street
WC2E 7AH

**Bow Street Magistrates'
Court**
WC2E 7AS

British Academy
SW1Y 5AH
britac.ac.uk

British Museum
WC1B 3DG
britishmuseum.org

Brompton Cemetery
SW10 9UG
royalparks.org.uk/parks/
brompton-cemetery

Buckingham Palace
SW1A 1AA
royal.gov.uk/theroyalresidences
/buckinghampalace/
buckinghampalace.aspx

Café Royal
W1B 4DY
hotelcaferoyal.com

Charing Cross Station
WC2 5HS

Charterhouse Square
EC1M 6AN
thecharterhouse.org

Chinatown
W1D 6JN
chinatownlondon.org

Christie's
SW1Y 6QT
christies.com

Coal Hole, The
WC2R 0DW
nicholsonspubs.co.uk/thecoal
holestrandlondon

**College of Psychic
Studies, The**
SW7 2EB
collegeofpsychicstudies.co.uk

Criterion
W1J 9HP
criterionrestaurant.com

Crystal Palace Park
SE19 2GA

Downing Street
SW1A
gov.uk/government/
organisations/prime-
ministers-office-10-downing-
street

Duke of York Steps
SW1Y 5AJ
royalparks.org.uk/parks/
st-jamess-park/things-to-see-
and-do/monuments-
fountains-and-statues/duke-
of-york-statue

Endell Street
WC2H 9AJ

Fenton House
NW3 6SP
nationaltrust.org.uk/fenton-
house

Fortnum & Mason
W1A 1ER
fortnumandmason.com

Freemasons' Hall
WC2B 5AZ
freemasons-hall.co.uk

George Inn, The
SE1 1NH
www.george-southwark.co.uk

Gieves & Hawkes
W1S 3JR
gievesandhawkes.com

Great Scotland Yard
SW1A

Grosvenor Square
W1K 2HP
grosvenor.com/featured-
locations-and-properties/
asset/grosvenor-square

Hampstead Heath
N6 4JH

Henry Poole & Co.
W1S 3PJ
henrypoole.com

Hunterian Museum
WC2A 3PE
rcseng.ac.uk/museums/
hunterian

Hyde Park
W2 2UH
royalparks.org.uk/parks/
hyde-park

Inner Temple
EC4Y

James J Fox
SW1A 1ES
jjfoxpipes.co.uk

James Lock
SW1A 1EF
lockhatters.co.uk

John Lobb
SW1A 1EF
johnlobbltd.co.uk

Langham Hotel
W1B 1JA
langhamhotels.com/en/the-
langham/London

Leadenhall Market
EC3V 1LT

Lincoln's Inn Fields
WC2A 3TL

London Bridge Station
SE1 9SP
www.networkrail.co.uk/
london-bridge-station

London Zoo
NW1 4RY
www.zsl.org/zsl-london-zoo

Lyceum Theatre
WC2E 7RQ
lyceumtheatrelondon.org

Marylebone Station
NW1 6JJ

Middle Temple Lane
EC4Y

Museum Tavern
WC1B 3BA
taylor-walker.co.uk/
pub/museum-tavern-
bloomsbury

National Gallery
WC2N 5DN
nationalgallery.org.uk

Natural History Museum
SW7 5BD
nhm.ac.uk

Nelson's Column
WC2N 5DU
london.gov.uk/priorities/arts-
culture/trafalgar-square/
visiting-trafalgar-square/
statues-and-fountains

**Norman Shaw Buildings
(formerly New Scotland
Yard)**
SW1A 2HZ

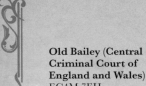

Old Bailey (Central Criminal Court of England and Wales)
EC4M 7EH
cityoflondon.gov.uk/about-the-city/about-us/buildings-we-manage/Pages/central-criminal-court.aspx

Old Royal Naval College
SE10 9NN
ornc.org

Palace of Westminster
SW1A 0AA
parliament.uk/about/living-heritage/building/palace

Pall Mall
SW1Y

Reform Club
SW1Y 5EW
reformclub.com

Regent's Park
NW1 4NR
royalparks.org.uk/parks/the-regents-park

Royal Albert Hall
SW7 2AP
royalalberthall.com

Royal Courts of Justice
WC2A 2LL
justice.gov.uk/courts/rcj-rolls-building

Royal Exchange
EC3V 3DG

Royal Observatory
SE10 8XJ
rmg.co.uk/royal-observatory

Royal Opera House
WC2E 9DD
roh.org.uk

Rules
WC2E 7LB
rules.co.uk

Russell Square
WC1B

St Bartholomew's Hospital and Museum
EC1A 7BE
bartshealth.nhs.uk

St James's Park
SW1A
royalparks.org.uk/parks/st-jamess-park

St James's Street
SW1A

St Mary-le-Bow
EC2V 6AU
stmarylebow.co.uk

St Pancras Renaissance London Hotel
NW1 2AR
marriott.co.uk/hotels/travel/lonpr-st-pancras-renaissance-london-hotel

St Pancras Station
N1C 4QP
stpancras.com

St Paul's Cathedral
EC4M 8AD
stpauls.co.uk

St Sepulchre-without-Newgate
EC1A 2DQ
stsepulchres.org

Savile Row
W1S

Savoy Theatre
WC2R 0ET
savoytheatre.org

Science Museum
SW7 2DD
sciencemuseum.org.uk

Shaftesbury Avenue
W1D

Sherlock Holmes Museum
NW1 6XE
sherlock-holmes.co.uk

Sherlock Holmes, The (pub)
WC2N 5DB
sherlockholmespub.com

Simpson's-in-the-Strand
WC2R 0EW
simpsonsinthestrand.co.uk

Somerset House
WC2R 1LA
somersethouse.org.uk

Speedy's Sandwich Bar & Café
NW1 2NJ
speedyscafe.co.uk

Stanfords
WC2E 9LP
stanfords.co.uk

Sweetings
EC4N 4SF

Tapas Brindisa
W1F 7AF
brindisa.com

Temple
EC4Y

Tower Bridge
SE1 2UP
towerbridge.org.uk

Tower of London
EC3N 4AB
hrp.org.uk/TowerOfLondon

Trafalgar Square
WC2N 5DN
london.gov.uk/priorities/arts-culture/trafalgar-square

Trafalgar Tavern
SE10 9NW
trafalgartavern.co.uk

Warren House
KT2 7HY
warrenhouse.com

Waterloo Station
SE1 8SW

Westminster Bridge
SW1A 2JH

Whitechapel Bell Foundry
E1 1DY
whitechapelbellfoundry.co.uk

Whitehall
SW1A

William Evans
SW1A 1PH
williamevans.com

Wilton's Music Hall
E1 8JB
wiltons.org.uk

INDEX

PICTURE CREDITS

Front cover map: Getty Images/Heritage Images; silhouette by Harriet de Winton © CICO Books. Page **1** Getty Images/Photo by FJ Mortimer; **2/3** Getty Images/Photo by FJ Mortimer; **3** Rex Features/ITV; **4** Getty Images/The LIFE Picture Collection; **5** Getty Images/Topical Press Agency; **6** Getty Images/General Photographic Agency; **8** Getty Images/Popperfoto; **9** Getty Images/SSPL; **10** Getty Images/Guildhall Library & Art Gallery/Heritage Images; **11 top** Alamy/ © The Keasbury-Gordon Photograph Archive; **11 bottom** Getty Images/Nichola Sarah; **12** Getty Images/Ann Ronan Pictures/Print Collector; **13** Mirrorpix/Brian Mackness ; **14** Getty Images/Photo byFJ Mortimer; **17** Alamy/ © Heritage Image Partnership Ltd; **18** Getty Images/Bob Thomas/Popperfoto; **19** Getty Images/Popperfoto; **21** Getty Images/SSPL; **22/23** Getty Images/Bob Thomas/Popperfoto; **24** Getty Images/Photo by FJ Mortimer; **25** Alamy/INTERFOTO; **28** Getty Images/Dan Kitwood; **29** Mary Evans Picture Library/ Antiquarian Images; **30** Alamy/John Kellerman; **31** Alamy/Chronicle; **32** © PHOTOGRAPH BY Pacific Coast News / Barcroft Media; **33** Corbis/Peter Aprahamian; **35** Alamy/age fotostock; **36 left** Alamy/ age fotostock; **36 right** Alamy/Peter Wheeler; **37** Corbis/Peter Aprahamian; **38** Corbis/ Bob Krist; **40** Getty Images/London Stereoscopic Company; **42** Alamy/ David South; **43** Getty Images/Keystone/Hulton Archive; **44/45** Getty Images/London Stereoscopic Company/Hulton Archive; **46** Alamy/INTERFOTO; **47** © Museum of London; **48** Corbis; **49 left** Corbis/ adoc-photos; **49 right** The Evans Skinner Crime Archive; **52** Alamy/Classic Image ; **53** Mirrorpix/Brian Mackness; **54** Alamy/Marcin S. Sadurski; **55** Getty Images/Guildhall Library & Art Gallery/Heritage Images; **56** Alamy/WENN Ltd ; **57 top** Mirrorpix; **57 bottom** Scott Grummett; **58** Alamy/Mary Evans Picture Library; **59** Wellcome Library, London; **60** Getty Images/SSPL; **61 left** Corbis/ adoc-photos; **61 right** Alamy/Photos 12 ; **64** Alamy/ Lebrecht Music and Arts Photo Library; **65** Alamy/ Visions of America, LLC; **66** Alamy/ Lordprice Collection; **67** Alamy/ The Art Archive ; **68** Alamy/Amoret Tanner; **69** Getty Images/Hulton Archive; **71** Getty Images/LL/Roger Viollet; **72** Alamy; **73** Getty Images/Graham Barclay/Bloomberg; **74** Getty Images/ Museum of London/Heritage images; **75** Getty Images/ Museum of London/Heritage images; **76 left** Getty Images/Imagno; **76 right** Getty Images/ Time Life Pictures/Mansell/The LIFE Picture Collection; **77** Alamy/Pictorial Press; **80/81** Alamy/The Print Collector; **82** Mary Evans Picture Library/The Wentworth Collection; **84/85** Getty Images/Culture Club; **85 right** Corbis/Hulton-Deutsch; **86** Topfoto; **87** Getty Images/ English Heritage/Heritage Images; **88** Mary Evans Picture Library; **89** Getty Images/London Stereoscopic Company; **90** Alamy/Lordprice Collection; **91** Getty Images/George De Keerle; **94** Alamy/Liszt collection; **96 left** Alamy/Chronicle; **96/97** Getty Images/Edward Gooch; **98** Alamy/Chronicle; **99** Alamy/Stephan Morris; **100** Getty Images/Last Refuge; **101** Alamy/Pictorial Press Ltd; **102/103** Alamy/The Natural History Museum; **104** Alamy/Arcaid Images; **105** Alamy/AF Archive; **106 left** TopFoto; **106 right** Alamy/Chronicle; **107** TopFoto; **108** Getty Images/Paul Popper/Popperfoto; **109** Mary Evans Picture Library/Everett Collection; **112** Getty Images/Science & Society Picture Library; **113** Getty Images/Topical Press Agency; **114** Getty Images/Hulton Archive; **115** © Museum of London; **117** Getty Images/Science & Society Picture Library; **119** Getty Images/Science & Society Picture Library; **120** Alamy/MS Bretherton; **121** Getty Images/Latitude Stock/David Williams; **122** Picture Desk/Silver Pictures/The Kobal Collection; **123** Getty Images/Heritage Images; **125** Getty Images/John Lawson, Belhaven; **126/127** Getty Images/ND/Roger Viollet; **127 right** Alamy/Heritage Image Partnership Ltd; **128** Alamy/picturelibrary; **129 left** Alamy; **129 right** Getty Images/Hutlon Archive; **130** Getty Images/Imagno; **131** Getty Images/FPG/Hulton Archive; **132** Science & Society Picture Library/National Railway Museum; **135** Getty Images/Science & Society Picture Library; **136** Alamy/VintagePostCards; **137** Alamy/ Tricia de Courcy Ling; **139 left** Alamy/Mick Sinclair; **139 right** Getty Images/Science & Society Picture Library; **140** Alamy/TA Images; **141** Alamy/Atomic; **143** Mary Evans Picture Library; **144** Alamy/ The Keasbury-Gordon Photograph Archive; **145** Getty Images/Science & Society Picture Library; **146** Alamy/Photos 12; **148** Rex Features/ITV; **149** Alamy/Rod Collins; **150** Alamy/AF Archive; **151** Rex Features/ITV; **152** Alamy/Photos 12; **153** Mary Evans Picture Library/Photo Researchers.

Every effort has been made to contact copyright holders and acknowledge sources. Any omissions will be rectified in future printings, if brought to the publisher's attention.

ACKNOWLEDGMENTS

It has been a great pleasure to work on another book with Penny Craig and Alison Wormleighton, consummate editor and brilliantly incisive copy editor respectively. I would also like to thank publisher Cindy Richards and art director Sally Powell at CICO Books. Grateful thanks again to picture researcher Claire Gouldstone for finding such wonderfully evocative images, and to Paul Tilby for the stylish design of the pages and cover. Finally, thanks to Patricia Harrington at CICO for the production of such a good-looking book.